Henry Vaughan and the Usk Valley

Robert Macdonald's imaginary portrait of Henry Vaughan,
of whom no historical image is known to exist

Henry Vaughan
and the Usk Valley

edited by
Elizabeth Siberry
and Robert Wilcher

Logaston Press

LOGASTON PRESS
Little Logaston Woonton Almeley
Herefordshire HR3 6QH
www.logastonpress.co.uk

First published by Logaston Press 2016
Text copyright © the author of each chapter

ISBN 978 1 910839 02 7

All rights reserved. No part of this publication
may be reproduced, stored in a retrieval system,
or transmitted in any form or by any means,
electronic, mechanical, photocopying, recording
or otherwise, without the prior permission,
in writing, of the publisher.

Typeset by Logaston Press
and printed and bound in Poland by www.lfbookservices.co.uk

Contents

Foreword — vii

Henry Vaughan: a Biographical Introduction — ix

1 'Pure and endless light': Henry Vaughan in his Landscape — 1
Jeremy Hooker

2 'These mists, and black days': Henry Vaughan and the Civil Wars — 17
Robert Wilcher

3 'Then keep the ancient way!': Henry Vaughan and the Interregnum — 29
Robert Wilcher

4 'Then bless thy secret growth': Henry Vaughan and the Church — 43
Helen Wilcox

5 'The truth and light of things': Henry Vaughan and Nature — 61
Jonathan Nauman

6 'New Cordials, new Cathartics': Henry Vaughan the Physician — 79
Simone Thomas

7 'Such low & forgotten thinges': the Vaughan Heritage — 87
Elizabeth Siberry

List of contributors — 101
Notes on the text — 102
Further reading — 103
Index — 107
Index of Henry Vaughan's poems — 110

Aerial photograph of the Usk Valley (courtesy of Getmapping plc)

Foreword

The seventeenth-century poet Henry Vaughan, also known as the Silurist, was born, lived most of his life and died in the Usk Valley near Brecon, in what is now the Brecon Beacons National Park, and his grave, at the church of St Bride's (Llansantffraed), is an important literary site. Here the anniversary of the poet's death on 23 April 1695 is celebrated by a special service each year, organized by Llansantffraed Church, in conjunction with the Brecknock Society and Vaughan Association. This annual event is a mark of the pride that local people take in Vaughan as a major Welsh poet and also of his wider fame in the literary world as one of the so-called Metaphysical Poets. People from throughout the world visit the area and are drawn to the poet's grave as part of their exploration of Brecknockshire's history and heritage, before crossing the river to Talybont to enjoy the Vaughan Walk, which celebrates his life and work.

Henry Vaughan's international reputation is the broader context and his local significance provides the more immediate motivation for this book, which was conceived during discussions between the Brecknock Society and the Vaughan Association in the spring of 2014 and marks another stage in the fruitful partnership between these organizations.

There have been numerous editions of and commentaries on Vaughan's poems and a short illustrated book, linking Vaughan's poems with photographs of the local landscape, was published by Helen Gichard and the Brecknock Society in 1995. In the intervening twenty years, however, much has been written about Vaughan and about the history of the area during the seventeenth century. The time therefore is right for a more detailed examination of his life and poetry in relation to the landscape and the historical situation in which he lived and worked and which provided the political impulse and spiritual inspiration for his writing.

Vaughan's poetry is not always easy to understand on first reading, so the poems that have been chosen as further illustrations of the topic of each chapter are supplied with explanatory notes and brief commentaries. For readers who wish to take their interest in Vaughan further, there is also a detailed list of books and articles at the end of the volume, which picks up references to secondary works cited in the text.

The chapters take a thematic approach, starting with a brief biographical introduction, followed by chapters on Vaughan's relation to the landscape in which he passed his life; the impact on South Wales of the civil wars and interregnum of the mid-seventeenth century, because Vaughan wrote in tumultuous times for Britain, the county of Brecknockshire, and his own family;

the interest that Vaughan and his twin brother, Thomas, took in the natural world; and Vaughan's relationship with the persecuted and outlawed Church of England. In his later years, however, Vaughan was better known as a physician and Simone Thomas, herself a GP with strong Welsh connections, writes on Vaughan's medical career, drawing on a shorter article produced for the Brecon Cathedral Magazine by a local doctor, Philip Snow. The book concludes with a chapter on how Vaughan has been remembered both locally and by later poets and artists – his heritage. There is inevitably and appropriately some overlap between the chapters but they in turn provide a variety of perspectives on Henry Vaughan as a poet and physician which we hope will enrich further reading of his work and visits to Llansantffraed, Tretower (the ancestral home of his branch of the Vaughans), the Usk Valley, and the wider environs of the National Park.

A book celebrating the life and work of a poet who drew inspiration from his local landscape needs to be well illustrated, and there are a number of new photographs of views of the area, including some sites that inspired poems quoted in this volume, which would still be recognized by Vaughan. There are also photographs of some of those who have been most influential in the revival of local interest in Vaughan and reproductions of works by contemporary Welsh artists who have been inspired by his poetry.

Members of the Brecknock Society Executive Council, Mervyn Bramley, John Gibbs and Glyn Mathias, have been very helpful in shaping the book. We are also grateful to Glyn Mathias for allowing us to quote from his father Roland Mathias's work, to Cinnamon Press for permission to include one of the poems by the late Anne Cluysenaar, and to the estate of George Sassoon for permission to publish a poem by Siegfried Sassoon; all works inspired by visits to Vaughan's grave. Another local charity, the Brecknock Arts Trust, has helped pull together the illustrations for the book and we are most grateful to the artists Clive Hicks-Jenkins and Robert Macdonald for allowing us to publish images from their work inspired by Henry Vaughan. We would also like to thank the members of the Llansantffraed Church Committee for their continuing support. We hope that this book will encourage many to visit not only Vaughan's grave but also the church of St Bride's itself.

The photographs and other illustrations are attributed in the text itself but particular thanks are due to Philip Coyne for letting us use his photographs of the area and to the National Library of Wales and the Brecknock Museum for permission to reproduce several paintings of the church, by different hands, which have not previously been published and which give an indication of what the church may have looked like in Vaughan's day, before its restoration in the late nineteenth-century. We are also grateful to Brecon Town Council for permission to publish the mayoral portrait of Gwenllian Morgan and Getmapping plc for permission to use the aerial photograph of the Usk Valley.

Elizabeth Siberry and Robert Wilcher

Henry Vaughan:
a biographical introduction

Henry Vaughan (1621-95) belonged to the branch of the Vaughan family that had had its seat at Tretower Court since the mid-fifteenth century. Taking its name from a great round tower that was added to the adjacent Norman motte and bailey castle in the thirteenth century, this medieval house (now open to the public, courtesy of Cadw) is situated a few miles to the east of Bwlch, within the boundary of the ancient Welsh kingdom of Brycheiniog and close to the Roman route that is followed by the modern A40 as it runs to the north of the River Usk between Brecon and Abergavenny. The Vaughans of Tretower traced their ancestry back to Dafydd ap Llywelyn, the 'Davy Gam, esquire' listed among those slain at the Battle of Agincourt in Shakespeare's *Henry V*. Gam's daughter, Gwladys, had married Sir Roger Vaughan of Bredwardine in Herefordshire, and it was their son, another Sir Roger, who built the courtyard house at Tretower and passed it down the generations to William Vaughan, the poet's grandfather, who married Frances, a granddaughter of Henry, Earl of Worcester. Through the offspring of Gwladys's second marriage, to Sir William Herbert of Raglan, the Tretower Vaughans were distantly related to the seventeenth-century poet, George Herbert. When William Vaughan died in 1613,

Tretower Castle

The inner courtyard at Tretower Court

the ancestral home was inherited by his elder son, Charles. His younger son, Thomas, married Denise Morgan, daughter of David Morgan from the parish of Llansantffraed and heiress to a small estate near the village of Scethrog. It was in the farmhouse called Trenewydd (Newton), situated in the Usk Valley between Scethrog and St Bride's Church, that they raised their family. Denise gave birth to the twins, Henry and Thomas, in 1621 and to a third son, William, in 1628; there may also have been a daughter, whose name has not survived. A comment in some verses by their friend and neighbour, Thomas Powell – 'Not only your *faces*, but your *wits* are *twins*' – is taken as evidence that Henry and Thomas were identical; and by Thomas's own account, they were brought up speaking both Welsh and English. They attended the church of St Bride of Llansantffraed, a short walk along the main road from their home, where the rectors during their childhood were John Perrott (from 1597) and Andrew Watkins (from 1631).

From the age of eleven, the twins were taught by the Revd Matthew Herbert, rector of Llangattock, some nine miles from Newton and just across the river from Crickhowell. Described in a contemporary history as 'a noted schoolmaster', Herbert was revered by Henry (in a Latin poem) as 'the pride of our Latinity'; and in another set of Latin verses, the poet attributes his own posthumous reputation to the 'watchful wisdom' of his tutor, claiming him as a second father: 'Share then your pupil! let this brief life be / My father's, and that future life for thee' (Edmund Blunden's translation). An idyllic account of the six years he spent under Herbert's care is given in the pastoral poem 'Daphnis', which relates how he sat with other pupils beneath the 'goodly shelter' of an oak tree by the 'large rich streams' of the Usk and listened to the learned rector recite Welsh bardic poetry:

> And many times had old Amphion made
> His beauteous flock acquainted with this shade;
> A flock, whose fleeces were as smooth and white
> As those, the welkin shows in moonshine night.
> Here, when the careless world did sleep, have I
> In dark records and numbers nobly high
> The visions of our black but brightest bard
> From old Amphion's mouth full often heard.

Henry's brother, Thomas, also honoured their 'old Schoolmaster' in Latin verses and dedicated one of his published works to him. F.E. Hutchinson speculates that the twins may have owed 'their first interest in astrology and the occult, and even in alchemical experiment'[1] to him; and it is even more likely that he introduced them to the religious poetry of George Herbert, which was later to have a profound influence on Henry's own development as a poet.

In 1638, the twins were sent to Oxford to continue their education. Thomas was admitted to Jesus College on 4 May, matriculated in the following December, and was awarded his BA degree in February 1642. There is no official record of Henry's residence, but we have his own word for it that he spent some time studying in Oxford; and Jesus College was where the Welsh gentry sent their sons to gain some intellectual polish, if not necessarily to take a degree. Furthermore, it is stated in Anthony Wood's history of writers and bishops who had been educated at Oxford University that Henry Vaughan entered Jesus College in the autumn of 1638 and studied there for some two years. The college accounts show that Thomas was resident intermittently as a graduate scholar until February 1648 and his own published works suggest that later in the same year he moved to London, where he pursued his interests in hermetic philosophy and alchemical experiment with likeminded members of the 'Chymical Club'. Many years later, Henry recalled that his twin brother had been ordained as a minister of the Church of England by Bishop Mainwaring and installed as rector in their home parish of Llansantffraed. The previous incumbent had died in 1643 or 1644, but Thomas Vaughan could not have replaced him until April 1645, when he reached the minimum age for ordination as a priest. Although a legal document refers to him as rector of Llansantffraed in the autumn of 1649, he may already have been deprived of his benefice along with other Anglican clergy by the Puritan authorities; and he was finally evicted in 1650, by which time he was fully committed to his hermetic writings and his chemical research in London. In the meantime, Henry had left Oxford without taking a degree and by 1640 was studying Law in the capital. These studies were interrupted by the outbreak of civil war between Parliament and Charles I in August 1642 and he returned to Breconshire at his father's behest. Both twins bore arms for the king, Thomas as a captain and Henry as a lieutenant in a troop of cavalry and both took part in a battle near Chester in September 1645 (see Chapter Two).

In 1646, Henry Vaughan published a small collection of original poems and a translation of a Roman satire; and by December 1647, he had prepared another collection of his early verses for the press. Publication of this second volume was delayed, however, probably due to the insurgency in Wales that was part of the Second Civil War of 1648 and more certainly by the death of his younger brother, William, in July. At this time, Henry also underwent a spiritual awakening, which he would later attribute to the 'holy life and verse' of George Herbert, pastor of Bemerton in Wiltshire, whose influential collection of religious verse, *The Temple*, had appeared posthumously in 1633. As a result of this 'conversion', Henry began to devote his talent to the devotional poetry for which he is chiefly remembered and in 1650 published the first part of *Silex Scintillans* (The Flashing Flint) with an engraved title-page that depicted a heart-shaped flint from which fire is being struck by a hand from heaven and tears or drops of blood are falling. Some of the poetry from the aborted volume of 1647, supplemented with translations in verse and prose, was finally seen into print as *Olor Iscanus* (The Swan of Usk) in 1651, probably by Henry's twin brother. Two volumes of prose followed: *The Mount of Olives: Or, Solitary Devotions* (1652) consisted of a manual of prayers for use by members of the Church of England in place of *The Book of Common Prayer*, which had been banned by the parliamentary regime, together with a meditation on death and the translation of a work attributed to St Anselm, Archbishop of Canterbury; and *Flores Solitudinis* (Flowers of Solitude), published in 1654, which contained translations of three religious treatises and a life of St Paulinus of Nola, all designed to help those who sought to withdraw from the temptations and troubles of the world into meditative solitude. A second part was added to *Silex Scintillans* in 1655; and two more prose translations, probably related to Vaughan's preparations for a career as a physician, were published in 1655 and 1657 (see Chapter Six). During the same period, Thomas Vaughan was at work on a series of tracts on hermetic philosophy: the first, *Anthroposophia theomagica*, was completed while he was still at Oxford in 1648 and published, along with *Anima magica abscondita*, in 1650; *Magia Adamica* followed later in the same year and *Lumen de lumine* in 1651, each accompanied by a controversial response to attacks on his occult ideas; *Aula lucis* appeared in 1652, and *Euphrates, or, The Waters of the East* in 1655. Several of these were published under his pseudonym, Eugenius Philalethes. Finally, in 1657, he wrote an introduction to his twin brother's translation of *The Chymists Key* by the physician and hermetic philosopher, Heinrich Nolle.

Probably in 1646, Henry Vaughan had married Catherine Wise, daughter of Richard Wise of Gilsdon Hall in Warwickshire, by whom he had a son and three daughters. After her death, at some time before the publication of the 1655 *Silex Scintillans*, he married her sister, Elizabeth Wise, who must have been helping to care for his children, and they added three more daughters and another son to the crowded eight-room family home at Newton. Henry became head of the household when his father died in 1658; Denise Vaughan survived her husband, but there is no record of her death. Thomas Vaughan, the younger twin, had also married, on 28 September 1651, but his wife – Rebecca Archer, daughter of Timothy Archer, rector of St Mary's in Meppershall, Bedfordshire – had no children and died in April 1658. Entries in a notebook in which Thomas Vaughan recorded his alchemical experiments indicate that she had been much more than a domestic partner or laboratory assistant, playing a full part in the iatrochemical research that Donald Dickson describes in the introduction to his edition of the notebook. It may have been an interest in the medical dimension of their work that led Henry towards the profession of a country doctor that he pursued throughout the later decades of his life.

At the Restoration of the monarchy and the Church of England in 1660, Thomas Vaughan made no attempt to be reinstated as rector of Llansantffraed and was employed, under the patronage of Sir Robert Moray, in the royal laboratory in Whitehall. It was Moray who paid for his burial at Albury, between Oxford and Thame, where he died in February 1666 while experimenting with mercury in a house in which they had set up their laboratory during the great plague of London. Henry included a reference to 'Noble *Murrey*' and his brother's final resting-place in his pastoral elegy, 'Daphnis', and in 1673 informed John Aubrey that he had prepared for the press a volume containing 'the Remaines of my brothers Latine Poems'. This volume, which also included some of his own unpublished original and translated verse, was eventually printed in 1678 under the title *Thalia Rediviva: The Pass-Times and Diversions of a Countrey-Muse*. In 1689, he and his second wife ceded the Newton farmhouse and estate to Thomas, the eldest of his eight children, and moved into a cottage in Scethrog. Henry Vaughan died on 23 April 1695 and was buried in the graveyard behind the church at Llansantffraed.

Extracts from Thomas Vaughan's poem on the River Usk, printed in his hermetic treatise Anima Magica Abscondita *(1650)*

> 'Tis day, my crystal Usk: now the sad night
> Resigns her place as tenant to the light.
> See the amazed mists begin to fly
> And the victorious sun hath got the sky.
> How shall I recompense thy streams, that keep
> Me and my soul awaked when others sleep?

I watch thy stars, I move on with the skies
And weary all the planets with mine eyes.
. . . .
What a clear, running crystal here I find:
Sure I will strive to gain as clear a mind,
And have my spirits – freed from dross – made light,
That no base puddle may allay their flight.
How I admire thy humble banks: nought's here
But the same simple vesture all the year.
I'll learn simplicity of thee …
Let me not live, but[1] I'm amazed to see
What a clear type[2] thou art of piety.
Why should thy floods enrich those shores, that sin
Against thy liberty and keep thee in?
Thy waters nurse that rude land which enslaves
And captivates thy free and spacious waves.
Most blessed tutors, I will learn of those
To shew my charity unto my foes,
And strive to do some good unto the poor,
As thy streams do unto the barren shore.
   All this from thee, my Ysca? Yes, and more;
I am for many virtues on thy score.[3]
Trust me[4] thy waters yet: why – wilt thou not so?
Let me but drink again and I will go.
I see thy course anticipates my plea:
I'll haste to God, as thou dost to the sea;
And when my eyes in waters drown their beams,
The pious imitations of thy streams,
May every holy, happy, hearty[5] tear
Help me to run to Heaven, as thou dost there.

[1] unless. [2] symbol. [3] in your debt. [4] entrust to me. [5] heartfelt.

The Vaughan twins may have written their respective poems to the River Usk in friendly competition. Henry (see Chapters One and Four) emphasises his ambition to emulate the long line of classical and modern poets and 'redeem' his native river 'from oblivious night'; Thomas wishes to 'recompense' it for the pleasing sound of its waters as he observes the night sky and for the lessons in humility, piety, charity, and penitence that he learns from its swift passage between its confining banks to the sea.

The Retreat

Happy those early days! when I
Shined in my Angel-infancy.

Before I understood this place
Appointed for my second race,[1]
Or taught my soul to fancy aught
But a white,[2] celestial thought,
When yet I had not walked above
A mile, or two, from my first love,[3]
And looking back (at that short space,)
Could see a glimpse of his bright face;
When on some *gilded cloud*, or *flower*
My gazing soul would dwell an hour,
And in those weaker glories spy
Some shadows of eternity;
Before I taught my tongue to wound
My conscience with a sinful sound,
Or had the black art to dispense
A several[4] sin to every sense,
But felt through all this fleshly dress
Bright *shoots* of everlastingness.
  O how I long to travel back
And tread again that ancient track!
That I might once more reach that plain,
Where first I left my glorious train,[5]
From whence the enlightened spirit sees
That shady city of palm trees;[6]
But (ah!) my soul with too much stay[7]
Is drunk, and staggers in the way.
Some men a forward motion love,
But I by backward steps would move,
And when this dust falls to the urn,
In that state I came return.

[1] the course of his life through this world. [2] this word often has its Welsh connotations of pure, happy, blessed in Vaughan's poetry. [3] Christ. [4] separate. [5] nineteenth-century critics compared this to the phrase 'trailing clouds of glory do we come' in Wordsworth's 'Immortality Ode'. [6] Jericho is called this in the Old Testament. [7] dwelling too long on earth.

This was the only one of Vaughan's poems selected by Francis Palgrave for inclusion in the first edition of *The Golden Treasury of English Verse* (1863). Its early popularity was partly due to supposed echoes of its conception of childhood in Wordsworth's 'Ode on the Intimations of Immortality'. The idea that the soul pre-exists its entry into the material world is found in hermetic writings.

'*Fair and young light!*'

Fair and young light! my guide to holy
Grief and soul-curing melancholy;
Whom living here I did still shun
As sullen night-ravens do the sun,
And led by my own foolish fire[1]
Wandered through darkness, dens and mire.
How am I now in love with all
That I termed then mere bonds[2] and thrall,
And to thy name, which still I keep,[3]
Like the surviving turtle,[4] weep!
O bitter cursed delights of men!
Our souls' diseases first, and then
Our bodies'; poisons that intreat
With fatal sweetness, till we eat;
How artfully do you destroy,
That kill with smiles and seeming joy?
If all the subtleties of vice
Stood bare before unpractised eyes,
And every act she[5] doth commence
Had writ down its sad consequence,
Yet would not men grant, their ill fate
Lodged in those false locks, till too late.
O holy, happy, healthy heaven,
Where all is pure, where all is even,
Plain, harmless, faithful, fair and bright,
But what earth breathes against thy light!
How blest had men been, had their *Sire*[6]
Lived still in league with thy chaste fire,
Nor made life through her long descents,[7]
A slave to lustful elements![8]
I did once read in an old book
Soiled with many a weeping look,
That the seeds of foul sorrows be
The finest things that are, to see.
So that famed fruit[9] which made all die
Seemed fair unto the woman's eye.
If these supplanters[10] in the shade
Of Paradise, could make man fade,
How in this world should they deter
This world, their fellow-murderer!
And why then grieve we to be sent
Home[11] by our first fair[12] punishment,
Without addition to our woes

And lingering wounds from weaker foes?
Since that doth quickly freedom win,
For he that's dead, is freed from sin.

O that I were winged and free
And quite undressed[13] just now with thee,
Where freed souls dwell by living fountains
On everlasting, spicy mountains!
    Alas! my God! take home thy sheep;
    This world but laughs at those that weep.

[1] will o' the wisp, which had the capacity to lead men astray. [2] a bitter play on the bond of marriage. [3] hold in solemn remembrance. [4] turtle-dove, a symbol of fidelity in marriage. [5] vice, personified as a temptress. [6] Adam, the first man. [7] down through the generations. [8] material things. [9] the apple eaten by Eve and then by Adam. [10] those who brought about the overthrow of humankind. [11] to heaven, by way of death, the punishment for original sin. [12] just, with perhaps a pun on 'the fair sex'. [13] having discarded the flesh, but perhaps with a pun on the common meaning.

This elegy is usually taken as a tribute to Vaughan's first wife, Catherine, whose death left him feeling guilty about the way he had failed to appreciate her goodness when she was alive. Alan Rudrum, in an essay on Vaughan's elegies, has suggested that the references to wandering 'through darkness, dens and mire' – lured by the 'cursed delights of men', the 'subtleties of vice', and 'false locks' – are Vaughan's confession of sexual infidelity; and that the diseases of the soul which lead to diseases of the body, and the 'fatal sweetness' which acts as a poison, allude to a sexually transmitted disease, either actual or feared. This personal sense of grief and shame is followed by a meditation on the consequences of the fall of Adam and Eve; and in the conclusion, the poet longs to leave this world and join his wife, now 'winged and free', in heaven.

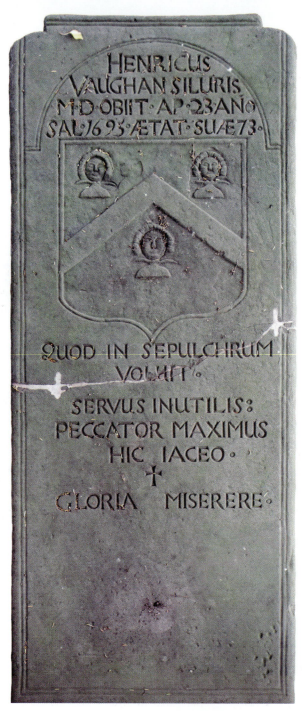

Henry Vaughan's gravestone at Llansantffraed (photograph Hywel Bevan)

For Norman & Deborah
'A quickness, which my God hath kissed'
love Jerry

1
'Pure and endless light': Henry Vaughan in his landscape

Jeremy Hooker

I

The title of *Olor Iscanus* (1651), Henry Vaughan's third published volume, styles the poet 'Swan of Usk'. In 'To the River Isca', he identifies himself with the river, which flowed in the valley below his home at Newton Farm:

> *Poets* (like *Angels*) where they once appear
> *Hallow* the *place*, and each succeeding year
> Adds *reverence* to't, such as at length doth give
> This aged faith, *that there their genii¹ live.*

¹ guardian spirits of place in classical poetry.

'This aged faith' places the poet in an ancient tradition of Roman pastoral poetry, which he combines with paying tributes to his contemporary poets. It is a self-consciously literary production. But the literary form of 'To the River Isca' does not invalidate the sincerity of its emotional content. Vaughan's poetry does hallow his native landscape. In other respects, too, the poem foreshadows the greater, original, work to come, in *Silex Scintillans*.

In 'To the River Isca', Vaughan requests that when at last he comes to be buried by the river (as he would be in the graveyard at Llansantffraed, close to his home):

> I'll leave behind me such a *large, kind light*,
> As shall *redeem* thee from *oblivious night*.

This in fact is what he achieved: the Usk's fame as a literary river is largely due to Henry Vaughan's poetry, through which it flows. Moreover, the imagery of 'a *large kind light*' looks forward to the light that illuminates his poetry. This is a light that he memorably described in 'The World (I)' as that 'great *Ring* of pure and endless light', the light of Eternity. But he did not apprehend it free of time, and somehow abstracted from history. Light in his poetry shines against surrounding darkness. 'To the River Isca' ends with Vaughan expressing the wish that the river's 'borders' be styled '*The land redeemed from all disorders!*'

Henry Vaughan's great poetry, in the first and the expanded editions of *Silex Scintillans*, is a response to disorders. These are at once personal and political: the death of his younger brother, his religious conversion as a broken man, his own serious illness, and the military triumph of Parliament over King Charles I. In the country around Newton, the churches were closed to the Anglican clergy and their congregations by the new officials appointed by the Puritan regime in London. From the family farmhouse, Vaughan looked out on a countryside in which the church he loved was closed, and the services which sustained him were unavailable (see Chapters Three and Four). In a prefatory letter to *Flores Solitudinis*, dated 17 April 1652, he depicts himself as writing 'out of a land of darkenesse', where his countrymen live 'in the shadow of death'. This is the darkness in and against which the light of *Silex Scintillans* shines.

Olor Iscanus, published after the first edition of *Silex Scintillans* but prepared for the press three years before it, is the work of a learned gentleman-poet, a man of classical education and tastes. There is little on the face of it that is distinctively Welsh about the book. It is possible, though, that Vaughan's self-designation, 'Swan of Usk', intends an allusion to a poem inspired by Llangorse Lake, 'The Swan of Syfadden Lake', ascribed to Dafydd ap Gwilym. Vaughan lived the greater part of his life not far from the lake, in a land of

A view up the Usk Valley from near Llansantffraed (photograph by Philip Coyne)

Welsh poetry, myth and legend. The countryside he and his twin brother grew up in was suffused with native magic. They were men who lived in two worlds in more than one sense. We may assume that for them classical education and local knowledge could easily coexist.

Some readers feel a peculiar intimacy with Henry Vaughan in his landscape. Louise Guiney pictured him travelling on horseback through the Welsh hills in his later role as physician. Anne Cluysenaar, in her poem-sequence 'Vaughan Variations', written in the 1990s, envisaged him, as he rides, discovering 'the clean grey branches of the ash / preparing their black buds, and in / a sheltered covert those hanging / dashes of hazel, loosening'.[2] For these and other readers, the poet is alive through his poems. He is a presence in his native landscape. To H.J. Massingham, a topographical writer with a poetic sensibility, Vaughan 'distills the spiritual essence of the Southern Marches'. Massingham, too, loved the landscape, of which he wrote:

> But it is not only his own Usk that the inward eye of the reader perceives flowing between the metrical banks of *Silex Scintillans*. When 'the pursie clouds disbande and scatter' from the aloof heads of the Black Mountains or the Brecon Beacons, when in some silent woodland of the Marches a noiseless wind stirs the tops of the trees and brushes back the mountain grasses or when the eye follows the combes and dingles winding their way into some pathless retreat, then I feel that none can interpret this strange country except the poet Vaughan.[3]

Llangorse Lake (photograph by Philip Coyne)

For such a reader, Henry Vaughan is the voice of his landscape. This is an understandable romantic impression, but it can hardly be accounted for by the poet's eye for topographical detail. Vaughan was not a local poet, a poet like Sir John Denham, author of *Cooper's Hill*, whose subject Samuel Johnson described as 'some particular landscape, to be particularly described'. Vaughan's landscape is much more inward. But it is not abstracted from the outer world. Rather, it is where outer and inner worlds meet, and spirit informs matter.

There are moments in Vaughan's poems when he awakes our senses to particular natural phenomena – flowers and trees and wild creatures, and effects of weather and seasons. In 'Regeneration', for example:

> The unthrift Sun shot vital gold
>   A thousand pieces,
> And heaven its azure did unfold
>   Chequered with snowy fleeces,
>   The air was all in spice
>   And every bush
> A garland wore; thus fed my eyes
>   But all the ear lay hush.

'The Shower (I)' suggests mist rising from Llangorse Lake:

> 'Twas so, I saw thy birth; that drowsy lake
> From her faint bosom breathed thee, the disease
> Of her sick waters, and infectious ease.

'Joy of my life! while left me here' shows us Vaughan's landscape in days before the A40 and speeding traffic passed Newton Farm on the way between Brecon and Abergavenny:

> Stars are of mighty use: the night
>   Is dark, and long;
> The road foul, and where one goes right,
>   Six may go wrong.

'The Water-fall' is a closely observed poem, catching the sight and sounds and rhythms of the moving water:

> With what deep murmurs through time's silent stealth
> Doth thy transparent, cool and watery wealth
>   Here flowing fall,
>   And chide, and call,
> As if his liquid, loose retinue stayed
> Ling'ring, and were of this steep place afraid ...

We cannot know whether this describes the falls at Blaen-y-Glyn on the Caerfanell River (subsequently dammed to form the reservoir above Talybont) or some other falls in the Brecon Beacons or Black Mountains. What we can know is that this is a poem of a man who lived most of his life in a country of waterfalls and loved to sit by them pensively with an observing eye.

The Vaughan twins' early fascination with water and light marks the work of both. As Thomas wrote: 'That which took me up much and soon, was the continual action of fire upon water.' Of this, he says: 'I will not forebear to write, how I had then fancied a certain practice upon water, out of which, even in those childish days, I expected wonders.' The alchemical philosophy of Thomas Vaughan may be said to have originated in his fascination with a natural phenomenon: sunlight shining on the waters of the Usk and other streams and rivers in the local landscape. The same wonderful phenomenon informs some of his brother's poems. In 'Midnight', Henry writes:

> Thy heavens (some say,)
> Are a firy-liquid light,
>   Which mingling aye
> Streams, and flames thus to the sight.
>   Come then, my god!
>   Shine on this blood,
> And water in one beam,
> And thou shalt see
>   Kindled by thee
> Both liquors burn, and stream.
>   O what bright quickness,
>   Active brightness,
> And celestial flows
>   Will follow after
>   On that water,
> Which thy spirit blows!

He appends to the poem a quotation from Matthew's Gospel, Chapter 3, verse 11, in which John the Baptist refers to Christ, for whom he prepares the way: '*I indeed baptize you with water unto repentance, but he that cometh after me is mightier than I, whose shoes I am not worthy to bear, he shall baptize you with the Holy Ghost, and with fire.*' The scriptural words refer us to the theology of baptism, which the poem has enacted in imagery of water and fire, and concentrated in 'a firy-liquid light'. 'Midnight' embodies a whole passionate thought-world. We may reflect that, like Thomas Vaughan's complex alchemical philosophy, this originated in a simple perception, as the boys observed the wonder of sunlight dyeing and streaming in the waters of the Usk.

II

The landscape of Henry Vaughan's poetry is a sacred landscape. What he shows us is life, in the sense of his poem, 'Quickness':

> But life is, what none can express,
> *A quickness, which my God hath kissed.*

This may be glossed by 'The Dedication', a poem addressed to Jesus Christ:

> Some drops of thy all-quickening blood
> Fell on my heart; those made it bud
> And put forth thus, though Lord, before
> The ground was cursed, and void of store.

His vision is of a fallen nature redeemed. His brother, the alchemist, has essentially the same vision: 'the *world* ... God's *building*, is full of *Spirit, quick*, and *living*'. It is an animate universe, a universe infused with spirit, that the Vaughan twins celebrate. In Henry's poetry this has a local habitation and a name.

In visiting his countryside today, in the Usk Valley and between the Brecon Beacons and the Black Mountains, this *quick* world is what we may perceive. It is the gift of a man of passionate loyalty, who identified politically with his native land as a voice of resistance to what he saw as its deadly enemies. In this respect his self-description as Silurist – related to an ancient British tribe that inhabited the Usk Valley – was crucial. It was an affirmation of identity. As Peter Thomas explains:

> As a direct descendant on Silures land, living not far from the site of a
> fierce and bloody action against the colonising Romans, he proclaims

The River Usk looking north-west (photograph by Philip Coyne)

both an inheritance of heroic guerrilla resistance, and his descent from the remnant of the 'true' ancient British Church driven into Wales over a thousand years earlier by the Saxon invasion.[4]

This history has a bearing on Vaughan's most famous lines, in 'The World (I)': 'I saw Eternity the other night / Like a great *Ring* of pure and endless light.' The ring of light is an image of universal order, which stands in opposition to the disorder of the mid-seventeenth century, a temporary condition in the context of eternity. Significantly, this is a vision of light seen at night, which for Vaughan, outdoors under the stars, was often the time of visionary seeing. His love of the world is not in question, as we see in his appreciation of trees and birds and other creatures, and of his native landscape, but he does not need to see it to love it, since his mind is on another world. Or, rather, he sees in earthly things the unearthly truth, and in the visible the invisible: Creation redeemed by Christ's 'all-quickening blood'.

This was not an abstract vision. It was in a special place that Henry Vaughan lived, and it was there that he wrote:

> They are all gone into the world of light!
>   And I alone sit ling'ring here;
> Their very memory is fair and bright,
>   And my sad thoughts doth clear.
>
> It glows and glitters in my cloudy breast
>   Like stars upon some gloomy grove,
> Or those faint beams in which this hill is dressed,
>   After the sun's remove.

'Here' is specific, justifying Joseph H. Summers' words on these lines: 'I do not know of an earlier passage in English poetry in which the reader is asked to respond to the details of a specific, privately-observed natural landscape ... as if the afterglow on *this* hill were different from that of any other.'[5] Certainly we may imagine Henry Vaughan sitting on The Allt, the hill rising immediately behind Newton Farm. With its views all round, this would have been an incomparable place from which to view the actual world; and at sunset, as the day's light faded, it would suggest withdrawal 'into the world of light'.

Something similar may be said about the particularity of 'The Water-fall':

> Dear stream! dear bank, where often I
> Have sat, and pleased my pensive eye,
> Why, since each drop of thy quick store
> Runs thither, whence it flowed before,
> Should poor souls fear a shade or night,
> Who came (sure) from a sea of light?

The bank, 'where often I / Have sat', is particular. It is liminal, also: not just a spot between land and water, but a situation between life and death, and time and eternity. The movements between outer and inner in both poems are similar. As the sun faded 'into the world of light', so souls, fearful of night, should be reassured by knowing that they 'came (sure) from a sea of light'. Vaughan's poems are characterised by flowing movements. In these two poems, we can see how physical, temporal phenomena image the flow of the seen into the unseen, and time into eternity.

III

In *The Mount of Olives* (1652), Vaughan advised: 'Look not upon transitorie, visible things, but upon him that is eternal, and invisible'. But, as a poet, Vaughan did look upon visible things, and in them perceived the invisible. His pastoral country of river valley and mountains was to his eye biblical, recalling places and stories from scripture. In the words of Stevie Davies:

> His poems are often accompanied by Biblical texts; and those texts may express themselves in a vision of landscape – Mount Horeb where God first spoke to Moses and Sinai where the Laws were given, the Mount of Olives, Mount Sion. Vaughan played these visionary mountains over the view of Pen y Bryn, Waun Rydd or Pen y Cader, and the ground of Brecknockshire acted as a mnemonic for the Holy Land.[6]

For Vaughan, Davies says, 'place is sacred because of its deep associations with Presence'; and Eluned Brown observes that the 'hallowed places' of the Bible 'are as much a part of his landscape as his own neighbourhood'.[7]

Vaughan's biblical landscape may seem distant from the twenty-first century. In recent years, however, he has been claimed as a 'green' poet, a poet with an ecological vision that speaks to the needs of our times. This may be said to constitute a movement, the main source of which is *Scintilla*, the annual journal of the Usk Valley Vaughan Association, first published in 1997. Poems and essays in this journal respond to Vaughan as a poet with an animate vision of nature. This may be seen in his sense of nature's flowing rhythms, and of process and colour, as in 'Affliction (I)':

> Were all the year one constant sun-shine, we
>   Should have no flowers,
> All would be drought, and leanness; not a tree
>   Would make us bowers;
> Beauty consists in colours; and that's best
>   Which is not fixed, but flies, and flows ...

Vaughan's poems in praise of a redeemed nature have at times a glorious liveliness. Thus, 'The Morning-Watch' evokes the response of the natural world to the coming of a new day:

> In what rings,
> And *hymning circulations* the quick world
> Awakes, and sings;
> The rising winds,
> And falling springs,
> Birds, beasts, all things
> Adore him in their kinds.
> Thus all is hurled
> In sacred *hymns*, and *order*, the great *chime*
> And *symphony* of nature.

This is one of Vaughan's finest lyrical poems, combining the energy of nature with a vision of universal order. Religious references, such as '*hymning circulations*', remind us that, with the Anglican church closed, the world is Vaughan's church, a building without walls, 'full of *Spirit, quick*, and *living*' (see Chapter Four). It is not too far-fetched, I think, to see an affinity between this jubilant sense of the sacred in the open air and the medieval Dafydd ap Gwilym's sanctification of the greenwood. This is not to claim that Vaughan read the older Welsh poet – he may or may not have done so. It is to point to a common spirit that may legitimately be described as Welsh.

Nature as Vaughan perceives it responds to the Creator. In 'The Bird' for example:

> All things that be, praise him; and had
> Their lesson taught them, when first made.
>
> So hills and valleys into singing break,
> And though poor stones have neither speech nor tongue,
> While active winds and streams both run and speak,
> Yet stones are deep in admiration.

All nature, including stones, recognizes Presence. With this vision, Vaughan's possible debt to Welsh poetry comes up for question again. Anne Cluysenaar, co-founder of *Scintilla*, makes a letter Vaughan wrote near the end of his life to John Aubrey the centrepiece of her 'Vaughan Variations'. Aubrey has asked Vaughan about the ancient Welsh Bards' *Awen* or gift of poetry, and Vaughan has responded with a story:

> I was told by a very sober & knowing person (now dead) that in his time, there was a young lad fatherless & motherless, & soe very poor that he was forced to beg; butt att last was taken vp by a rich man, that

kept a great stock of sheep vpon the mountains not far from the place where I now dwell, who cloathed him & sent him into the mountains to keep his sheep. There in the Summer time following the sheep & looking to their lambs, he fell into a deep sleep; In wch he dreamt, that he saw a beautifull young man with a garland of green leafs vpon his head, & an hawk vpon his fist: with a quiver full of Arrows att his back, coming towards him (whistling several measures or tunes all the way) & att last lett the hawk fly att him, w^{ch} (he dreamt) gott into his mouth & inward parts, & suddenly awaked in a great fear & consternation; butt possessed with such a vein, or gift of poetrie, that he left the sheep & went about the Countrey, making songs vpon all occasions, and came to be the most famous Bard in all the Countrey in his time.

Roland Mathias, a scrupulous historian of Vaughan's Brycheiniog and a fine poet, one of whose poems is 'On the Grave of Henry Vaughan at Llansantffraed', is sceptical of the interpretation of this letter as proof of Vaughan as a Welsh poet. 'What this letter really shows,' Mathias claims, 'is that Vaughan was either too tired to bother to answer Aubrey's query about the rules of the strict metres in Welsh ... or that he knew very little of them and that his story of the *Awen* or gift of poetry entering the mouth of a young shepherd boy while he lay asleep was diversionary cover of the kind he knew Aubrey would love.'[8] These are cautionary words. It may be that Vaughan's story relates to an ancient tradition associated with Orpheus and Myrddin rather than having anything to do with the strict metres. It may also be a story that for Vaughan expresses the Celtic spirit of his native landscape. But we should not think of Vaughan as a romantic poet. Rather we should be, like Roland Mathias, aware of what his theology meant to him. The words on Henry Vaughan's grave, SERVUS INUTILIS: PECCATOR MAXIMUS, mean what they say: 'A useless servant and the greatest of sinners'. He knew himself to be a fallen man in need of redemption, and he felt the need intensely: 'O knit me, that am crumbled dust!' ('Distraction'). But we should also remember that the letter tells a local story, a story about a landowner and a shepherd boy, 'upon the mountains not far from the place where I now dwell'. Vaughan knew that he lived in an ancient land, and from boyhood he and his twin brother had been responsive to wonders. As we read the letter, we may think of him looking back across his lifetime to boyhood days, when he may have first heard the story. Whether or not he intended to amuse Aubrey, he would have treasured the story as a tale belonging to his home ground. For us, it speaks of a 'green' spirit alive in Henry Vaughan's poetry and in his landscape: a spirit that remains to inspire others.

Upon the Priory Grove, His Usual Retirement

Hail sacred shades! cool, leafy house!
Chaste treasurer of all my vows,
And wealth! on whose soft bosom laid
My love's fair steps I first betrayed:[1]
   Henceforth no melancholy flight,
No sad wing, or hoarse bird of night,
Disturb this air, no fatal throat
Of raven, or owl,[2] awake the note
Of our laid Echo, no voice dwell
Within these leaves, but *Philomel*.[3]
The poisonous ivy here no more
His false twists on the oak shall score,
Only the woodbine here may twine,
As th' emblem of her love, and mine;
The amorous Sun shall here convey
His best beams, in thy shades to play;
The active air, the gentlest showers,
Shall from his wings rain on thy flowers;
And the Moon from her dewy locks
Shall deck thee with her brightest drops:
What ever can a fancy move,
Or feed the eye; be on this grove;
   And when at last the winds, and tears
Of Heaven, with the consuming years,
Shall these green curls[4] bring to decay,
And clothe thee in an aged grey:
(If aught a lover can foresee;
Or if we poets prophets be)
From hence transplanted, thou shalt stand
A fresh grove in the Elysian Land;[5]
Where (most blessed pair!)[6] as here on earth
Thou first didst eye our growth, and birth;
So there again, thou 'lt see us move
In our first innocence, and love:
And in thy shades, as now, so then,
We'll kiss, and smile, and walk again.

---

[1] revealed (meaning that his love for her was first declared there). [2] birds of ill omen. [3] the nightingale, which traditionally sings of love. [4] the foliage of the trees. [5] the abode of the blessed after death in Greek mythology. [6] the poet and his beloved.

The Priory Grove (photograph by Philip Coyne)

 This is the last of the original poems in Vaughan's first volume, *Poems with the Tenth Satire of Juvenal Englished* (1646). It follows a group of love poems addressed to 'Amoret' and is usually taken to be the triumphant conclusion of the poet's courtship of Catherine Wise, his first wife. The Priory Grove was a wooded area belonging to Brecon Priory, the home of Sir Herbert Price. Price had close connections with the Wise family from Coleshill in Warwickshire and it is likely that Vaughan first met Catherine when she was visiting the Priory. In the traditional manner of a poem celebrating betrothal or marriage, evil omens are banished from the place and blessings are called down upon it and the happy couple. In the final paragraph, Vaughan looks beyond the present to a future in which the grove will be transplanted to a realm beyond decay and death, where it will once again witness the innocent passion of the transfigured couple whose love first burgeoned beneath its shade.

Religion

   My God, when I walk in those groves,
   And leaves[1] thy spirit doth still fan,
   I see in each shade that there grows
   An Angel talking with a man.

   Under a *juniper*, some house,[2]
   Or the cool *myrtle's* canopy,
   Others beneath an oak's green boughs,

Or at some *fountain's* bubbling eye;
Here *Jacob* dreams, and wrestles; there
Elias by a raven is fed,
Another time by the Angel, where
He brings him water with his bread;

In *Abraham's* tent the winged guests
(O how familiar then was heaven!)
Eat, drink, discourse, sit down, and rest
Until the cool, and shady *even*;[3]

Nay thou thy self, my God, in *fire*,
Whirl-winds, and *clouds*, and the *soft voice*[4]
Speak'st there so much, that I admire[5]
We have no conference[6] in these days;

Is the truce broke? or 'cause we have
A mediator[7] now with thee,
Dost thou therefore old treaties[8] waive
And by appeals from him decree?

Or is't so, as some green heads[9] say,
That now all miracles must cease?
Though thou hast promised they should stay
The tokens of the Church, and peace;

The Priory Grove (photograph by Philip Coyne)

No, no; Religion is a spring
That from some secret, golden mine
Derives her birth, and thence doth bring
Cordials[10] in every drop, and wine;[11]

But in her long, and hidden course
Passing through the earth's dark veins,
Grows still from better unto worse,
And both her taste, and colour stains,

Then drilling on, learns to increase
False *echoes*, and confused sounds,
And unawares doth often seize
On veins of *sulphur*[12] under ground;

So poisoned, breaks forth in some clime,
And at first sight doth many please,
But drunk, is puddle, or mere slime
And 'stead of physic, a disease;

Just such a tainted sink we have
Like that *Samaritan's* dead *well*,[13]
Nor must we for the kernel crave
Because most voices like the *shell*.

Heal then these waters, Lord; or bring thy flock,
Since these are troubled, to the springing rock,[14]
Look down great Master of the feast; O shine,
And turn once more our Water into Wine![15]

Song of Solomon Chapter 4, verse 12
My sister, my spouse is a garden enclosed, as a spring shut up, and a Fountain sealed up.[16]

[1] both the leaves of trees referred to in the Old Testament and the pages of the Bible. [2] take shelter, like the prophet Elijah (1 Kings 19: 5). [3] all the foregoing are examples of angels engaging with prophets in the Old Testament. [4] God spoke to Moses and Job out of a burning bush, a cloud, and a whirlwind. [5] wonder or marvel. [6] conversation. [7] Christ. [8] covenants between God and humankind in the Old Testament. [9] not yet wise in counsel. [10] restorative drinks; [11] of Holy Communion (the blood of Christ); [12] associated with hell. [13] Christ offered a Samaritan woman at a well the 'living water' of salvation. [14] St Paul calls Christ the 'spiritual Rock' from which the water of salvation flows. [15] Christ turned water into wine at the marriage feast in Cana. [16] The Song of Solomon was traditionally read as an allegory of Christ's 'marriage' to the church.

This is a poem about the state of religion in the Britain of Vaughan's day, which is likened to a river that had its source in a pure spring giving refreshment (cordials) and salvation (wine), but has been contaminated by passing through the 'dark veins' of the material world and now offers false teaching and the outward shell of godliness (rather than the kernel of the Christian message). The first five stanzas illustrate the way in which the hallowed places of the Bible are as familiar to Vaughan as the features of his own Welsh landscape. The groves and streams of the Old Testament, through which he imagines himself walking, were the setting for close contact between angels and human beings. Such familiarity, however, is no longer possible now that the well of religion is a tainted sink and the river that flows from it mere puddle and slime. In the final stanza, he calls upon Christ to restore by miracle the true gospel of the New Testament as he once turned water into wine in a feast that looked forward to the Eucharist.

The Dawning

Ah! what time wilt thou come? when shall that cry
    The *Bridegroom's coming*![1] fill the sky?
Shall it in the evening run
When our words and works are done?
Or will thy all-surprising light
    Break at midnight?
When either sleep, or some dark pleasure
Possesseth mad man without measure;
Or shall these early, fragrant hours
    Unlock thy bowers?
And with their blush of light descry[2]
Thy locks crowned with eternity;
Indeed, it is the only time
That with thy glory doth best chime,
All now are stirring, every field
    Full hymns doth yield,
The whole Creation shakes off night,
And for thy shadow looks the light,
Stars now vanish without number,
Sleepy planets set, and slumber,
The pursy[3] clouds disband, and scatter,
All expect some sudden matter,
Not one beam triumphs, but from far
    That morning-star.

O at what time soever thou
(Unknown to us,) the heavens wilt bow,

And, with thy Angels in the *van*,[4]
Descend to judge poor careless man,
Grant, I may not like puddle lie
In a corrupt security,
Where, if a traveller water crave,
He finds it dead, and in a grave;
But as this restless, vocal *spring*[5]
All day, and night doth run, and sing,
And though here born, yet is acquainted
Elsewhere,[6] and flowing keeps untainted;
So let me all my busy age
In thy free services engage,
And though (while here) of force[7] I must
Have commerce sometimes with poor dust,
And in my flesh, though vile, and low,
As this[8] doth in her channel, flow,
Yet let my course, my aim, my love,
And chief acquaintance be above;[9]
So when that day, and hour shall come
In which thy self will be the Sun,[10]
Thou'lt find me dressed and on my way,
Watching the break of thy great day.[11]

[1] Christ, the bridegroom of the church, will return to judge the world on the last day. [2] announce. [3] swollen, heavy. [4] as an advance guard. [5] an actual stream in the Usk Valley. [6] that is, with a spiritual realm. [7] of necessity. [8] like this pure stream. [9] with heavenly things. [10] the Son of God, bringing the light of eternity on the last day. [11] Judgement Day.

Like many people in the turbulent years of the mid-seventeenth century, Vaughan believed that he was living through the 'last times' before the end of the world. In this meditation, he argues that the most appropriate time for the Second Coming of Christ would be the moment of dawn. The first half of the poem culminates in one of Vaughan's most beautiful evocations of a natural scene – more a skyscape than a landscape – which directs our attention to the changing appearance of the heavens, as the stars fade from sight and the bank of cloud breaks up, until only Venus, the morning star, remains visible and sunlight begins to flood over the earth. In the second half, he prays that he will be found a worthy servant of God, already dressed and eager for the journey from the night of time into the light of eternity.

2

'These mists, and black days': Henry Vaughan and the Civil Wars

Robert Wilcher

I

Henry Vaughan wrote to John Aubrey on 15 June 1673 that 'I stayed not at Oxford to take any degree, butt was sent to London, beinge then designed by my father for the study of the Law'. His move from Oxford to the capital in 1640 had brought him into direct contact with national politics. It was a stirring time to be there: the Scots, in rebellion against the religious policy of Charles I, occupied England's northern counties in August 1640; a Puritan mob broke up a session of the Court of Commission with cries of 'No bishop!' in October; and the Long Parliament that would eventually take up arms against the king assembled on 3 November. The rift between the two sides widened and a propaganda war was waged during the first half of 1642. The raising of the royal standard at Nottingham on 22 August signalled not only the beginning of military hostilities but also the end of Vaughan's sojourn in London. As he would put it in the letter to Aubrey, his further education was 'wholie frustrated' by 'the sudden eruption of our late civil warres'.

Some months before open war was declared, Parliament passed a Militia Ordinance, which gave it the power to summon the county trained bands; and the king revived commissions of array, an ancient means of recruiting troops to serve the crown. The most positive response to Charles I's call to arms came from a long strip of territory in the west of England, from the south-west up through the Welsh Marches to Lancashire, so that by the end of August Royalists controlled the greater part of the counties of Cornwall, Hereford, Monmouth, Worcester, Shropshire and Cheshire. Across the border, commissions of array were held by the Members of Parliament for Breconshire, William Morgan and Herbert Price, and by several other members of the local gentry, including John Jeffreys of Abercynrig and Vaughan's cousin, Charles Walbeoffe of Llanhamlach. Apart from Pembrokeshire, which remained committed to the cause of Parliament, the Welsh counties were an important source of manpower for the Royalist armies throughout the Civil War. A large number of Welsh troops fought for the king in the first major battle at Edgehill on 23 October. Breconshire itself saw no significant military action, but Herbert Price, who lived in the old Benedictine priory in Brecon, was not only one of the king's commissioners but also colonel of a regiment of horse. F.E. Hutchinson describes him as 'the most active and continuously loyal supporter of the royal arms in the county of Brecon'.[9] He was acting governor of Hereford when the city was compelled to surrender to a Parliamentary army in April 1643. A year later, he was back in Brecon raising troops to assist the Royalists of Carmarthen and Cardigan in their efforts to keep the Parliamentary force led by Colonel Rowland Laugharne bottled up in Pembrokeshire.

The only indication we have of Henry Vaughan's activities after his return home at the outbreak of war is the somewhat vague remark by Aubrey that 'he was a Clarke sometime to Judge Sir Marmaduke Lloyd'.[10] This occupation, presumably gained on the strength of his legal studies in London, must have meant a good deal of travelling, since Lloyd was Chief Justice of the Brecon Circuit, which took in Brecon, Radnor and Glamorgan. It cannot have continued beyond December 1645, when Lloyd – an active supporter of the king – was discharged from office, having been taken prisoner when Hereford was again captured by a Parliamentary force. By then, Vaughan had also experienced military service. The external evidence for this (outside his own poetry) is the appearance of his name on a list of former Royalist officers claiming relief for expenses incurred during the Civil Wars. This official document, dated 4 February 1663, also includes the names of Sir Herbert Price and Captain Thomas Vaughan, Henry himself being listed as lieutenant to Captain Barth. He had probably served in Price's regiment, which was involved in a battle near Chester on 24 September 1645. It is possible that he had enlisted earlier than this, but the only certain details of his military career are that he took refuge in Beeston Castle after the defeat at Rowton Heath and was among those permitted to march out unmolested when the garrison surrendered on 16 November.

Between 1642 and 1645, while Vaughan was at home writing poetry or out and about with Sir Marmaduke Lloyd, the war had ebbed and flowed inconclusively along the border between England and Wales. Further afield, however, the tide began to turn against the king. The major reverse at Marston Moor on 2 July 1644 was quickly followed by the loss of York and the north. Parliament's recently established New Model Army, under the command of Sir Thomas Fairfax and Oliver Cromwell, won a decisive victory against Prince Rupert on 14 June 1645 at Naseby, where the king's Welsh infantry suffered heavy losses. Charles I withdrew to South Wales on a recruiting drive, making his headquarters at Raglan Castle, the seat of the Marquis of Worcester, one of his major supporters. After a fruitless journey to Cardiff, the royal party trekked back across the Brecon Beacons and the king spent the night of 5 August with Colonel Price at the former priory. Leaving Brecon by way of the King's Steps, Charles travelled north through Radnorshire, then doubled back to relieve Hereford, which was once more being besieged, this time by a Scottish army. By 7 September he was back at Raglan Castle. It was most likely during those hectic months when the king himself was frequently in the neighbourhood of Brecon and Colonel Price was doing his best to make good the Royalist losses suffered at Naseby that Vaughan took the step of enlisting in a troop of cavalry. In the autumn of 1645, he found himself riding north to the defence of Chester, since one of the king's main priorities at this juncture of the war was to keep control of that city. It was the last port in the west still in Royalist hands and the only chance of receiving desperately needed reinforcements from Ireland. What the twenty-four-year-old Vaughan went through during and after the Battle of Rowton Heath was graphically recorded in two of the poems that were subsequently published in *Olor Iscanus* (1651).

The first poem – an elegy for a friend, known only by the initials R.W. – begins by explaining that the poet has endured 'a full year's grief' before accepting that this young man, not quite twenty years old, is dead. He recalls vividly how he lost sight of him in the heat and smoke of the battle, which gave him the hope that he might have come through the ordeal unscathed and been taken prisoner. Now, however, he has to accept that R.W.'s bravery was such that he would have preferred to die fighting than submit to captivity:

>   O that day
> When like the *fathers* in the *fire* and *cloud*[1]
> I missed thy face! I might in every *crowd*
> See arms like thine, and men advance, but none
> So near to lightning moved, nor so fell on.
>   ... like *shot* his active hand
> Drew blood, ere well the foe could understand.
> But here I lost him. Whether the last turn
> Of thy few sands[2] called on thy hasty urn,[3]
> Or some fierce rapid fate (hid from the eye)
> Hath hurled thee prisoner to some distant sky
> I cannot tell, but that I do believe
> Thy courage such as scorned a base reprieve.[4]

[1] In the Old Testament, God concealed himself in cloud and fire (See Exodus 24: 15-17). [2] the hourglass that measured R.W.'s life. [3] funeral urn for his ashes. [4] from death.

The other, more light-hearted, poem was born of the camaraderie rather than the tragic losses of war. Entitled 'Upon a Cloak Lent Him by Mr J. Ridsley', it thanks a friend for the loan of a grotesquely voluminous garment that afforded him welcome shelter from the elements when he marched out of Beeston Castle two months after the disaster at Rowton Heath:

> Hadst thou been with me on that day, when we
> Left craggy *Beeston*, and the fatal *Dee*,
> When beaten with fresh storms, and late mishap
> It shared the office of a *cloak*, and *cap*,
> To see how 'bout my clouded head it stood
> Like a thick *turband*, or some lawyer's *hood*,
> While the stiff, hollow pleats on every side
> Like *conduit-pipes*¹ rained from the *bearded hide*,
> I know thou wouldst in spite of that day's fate
> Let loose thy mirth at my new shape and state,
> And with a shallow smile or two profess
> Some *Sarazin*² had lost the *clouted*³ *dress*.

¹ drainpipes. ² Saracen. ³ patched.

Although he can share the funny side of his situation with a friend, this account of the comic figure he cut on 'that day' beside the 'fatal *Dee*' near Chester is a way of coping with the serious consequences of an event which helped to seal the 'fate' of the king's cause in the Welsh Marches.

II

When Vaughan was besieged in Beeston Castle, Major-General Laugharne had been advancing from his stronghold in Pembroke across South Wales towards Brecon. The townspeople, rather than preparing to resist, had written to him to forestall violence; and, as Richard Symonds (a royal lifeguard, who had accompanied Charles I on his march north to Chester) recorded in his diary on 12 November, they 'had pulled down the castle of Brecknock, and walls of the town'.[11] When Laugharne arrived on 23 November, he was greeted with a declaration signed by the sheriff of Brecon and thirty-three of the local gentry in which they submitted to Parliament and repudiated their previous allegiance to the king. Vaughan's disgust at this craven act of capitulation can be seen in a poem that he wrote some time over the winter of 1645-46. 'To His Retired Friend, an Invitation to Brecknock' was probably addressed to a former comrade in Price's regiment, since it includes his horse in the opening reproach that his friend has 'not so much as drunk, or littered here' for some time. Vaughan combines a gesture towards the Cavalier pastime of carousing with bitter observations on the changed circumstances that his drinking companion will encounter if he comes to Brecon:

> What ever 'tis, a sober cause't must be
> That thus long bars us of thy company.
> The town believes thee lost, and didst thou see
> But half her sufferings, now distressed for thee,
> Thou'ldst swear (like Rome) her foul, polluted walls
> Were sacked by *Brennus*, and the savage *Gauls*.[1]
> Abominable face of things! here's noise
> Of banged mortars, blue aprons,[2] and boys,
> Pigs, dogs, and drums, with the hoarse hellish notes
> Of politicly-deaf usurers' throats,
> With new fine *Worships*, and the old cast *team*
> Of Justices vexed with the *cough*, and *phlegm*.
> Midst these the *Cross*[3] looks sad, and the *Shire-Hall* furs of an old *Saxon Fox* appear,
> With brotherly ruffs and beards, and a strange sight
> Of high monumental hats ta'en at the fight
> Of *Eighty-eight*;[4] while every *Burgess*[5] foots
> The mortal *pavement* in eternal boots.[6]

[1] Brennus and the Gauls sacked Rome in 390BC. [2] tradesmen. [3] in the market-place. [4] the year of the Spanish Armada. [5] town councillor or magistrate. [6] mocking Puritan claims to godliness.

The Royalist poet pours scorn upon 'the new fine *Worships*' (municipal officials appointed by the victorious Parliamentarians) and the townsfolk who strut through the noisy streets in the old-fashioned garb favoured by Puritans. Particular venom is reserved for the 'old *Saxon Fox*' (an Englishman named John Eltonhead, who had replaced Vaughan's former employer as Chief Justice of the Brecon Circuit), wrapped in the furs that denote his exalted position. The only consolation the poet can offer his friend if he accepts his invitation is the defeated Royalist resource of drowning sorrow in drink and keeping out the cold of the last winter of war with merry companionship and contempt for the foolish and money-grubbing victors:

> Come then! and while the slow icicle hangs
> At the stiff thatch, and winter's frosty pangs
> Benumb the year, blithe (as of old) let us
> 'Midst noise and war, of peace, and mirth discuss.[1]
> This portion thou wert born for: why should we
> Vex at the time's ridiculous misery?
> An age that thus hath fooled it self, and will
> (Spite of thy teeth and mine)[2] persist so still.

> Let's sit then at this *fire*, and while we steal
> A revel in the town, let others seal,
> Purchase or cheat, and who can, let them pay,
> Till those black deeds[3] bring on the darksome day;[4]
> Innocent spenders we! a better use
> Shall wear out our short lease,[5] and leave the obtuse
> Rout to their *husks*; they and their bags[6] at best
> Have cares in *earnest*, we care for a jest.

[1] converse. [2] in spite of our resistance. [3] a pun on legal documents and actions. [4] the day of death. [5] the lease of life (another pun on legal terminology). [6] of money.

While Vaughan was kicking his heels at home, the disheartening news that Chester had fallen on 3 February 1646 came through. Even greater gloom must have been caused by the story of Charles I's flight from Oxford, dressed as a servant, on 27 April; and of his eventual surrender on 5 May to the Earl of Lothian, who was in command of the Scottish force laying siege to the Royalist garrison town of Newark. The poem Vaughan wrote on this occasion – 'The King Disguised' – expresses the shock of a devoted Royalist at the king's demeaning of his sacred person by adopting such a role and such garments:

> But I am vexed, that we at all can guess
> This change, and trust great *Charles* to such a dress.
> When he was first obscured with this coarse thing,
> He graced *plebeians*, but profaned the King.
> Like some fair Church, which zeal to charcoals burned,
> Or his own Court now to an ale-house turned.

In the final couplet of this extract, Vaughan underlines the extent to which church and state have been desecrated by the fanaticism of the triumphant Puritans. Later in the poem, he manages to salvage something of the mystique of kingship by persuading himself that the 'Royal Riddle' of Charles's action is one of the 'Secrets of State' that mere subjects must not pry into. But his reflections end uneasily with a warning about those to whom the king has entrusted his royal person:

> Be sure to look no Sanctuary there,
> Nor hope for safety in a temple, where
> Buyers and sellers[1] trade: O strengthen not
> With too much trust the treason of a Scot!

[1] an allusion to Christ's overthrowing of the tables of the traders in the temple at Jerusalem.

Such suspicion was well judged (or perhaps was added in a later revision), since the Scots soon moved the king to Newcastle, where they attempted to persuade him to introduce their system of Presbyterianism into the English church. When this failed, they sold him to Parliament for £400,000 in January 1647. Vaughan's uncomfortable poem was not published until 1678.

Charles remained in Parliament's custody at Holdenby House in Northamptonshire until June 1647, when he was abducted by Cornet Joyce (perhaps at the instigation of Cromwell) and became a prisoner of the Army. He was moved from place to place and in August ended up at Hampton Court, where he played off the Army against Parliament and opened secret talks with the Scots. In November, he escaped to the Isle of Wight, only to find himself confined in Carisbrooke Castle under the care of one of Cromwell's cousins. Unrest at the current state of affairs, with Army and Parliament at loggerheads, resulted in a series of armed risings on behalf of the king in 1648, which collectively constituted the Second Civil War. As early as June 1647, there had been disturbances in Glamorgan directed at the system of rule by county committees appointed by the authorities in London. These were the prelude to a more general Royalist insurgency in the north and south of Wales, which was joined by two former Parliamentary officers in Pembrokeshire – Colonel John Poyer and Major-General Laugharne – who had been alienated by the high-handedness of Parliament and its failure to make good arrears of pay for its veterans. Laugharne was heavily defeated by Colonel Horton at St Fagan's, the largest single battle of the Civil Wars on Welsh soil, and the two renegade officers finally surrendered to Cromwell on 11 July. Further afield, Vaughan lost another friend at the siege of Pontefract, which had been seized by a Royalist force in June and held out until March 1649. It was in a daring sally from the castle against the besieging army that 'Mr R. Hall' met the heroic end commemorated in the second of Vaughan's war elegies. Roland Mathias wonders whether four lines in particular contain the poet's guilty verdict on his own failure to participate in the Royalist action nearer home:

> Thus when some quitted action, to their shame,
> And only got a *discreet cowards* name,
> Thou with thy blood mad'st purchase of renown,
> And diedst the glory of the *Sword* and *Gown*.[1]

[1] Hall was a soldier and a clergyman.

Mathias may well be right that 'in lauding Hall the cowardice he speaks of ... is intendedly his own',[12] since Vaughan suffered a far greater loss in the summer of 1648, when his much-loved younger brother, William, died, probably from wounds received fighting for the king. Thomas Vaughan wrote that the youngster's death was the result of some 'glorious employment'; and Henry himself later complained in *The Mount of Olives* (1652) that 'furious and implacable' enemies had 'washed their hands in the blood of my friends, my dearest and nearest relatives'. Scattered through the two editions of *Silex Scintillans*, initially published in 1650 and augmented in 1655, are untitled elegies for William that chart the slow process of Henry's struggle with grief, from utter devastation that made life intolerable to acceptance and the courage to carry on.

'Silence and stealth of days'

Silence, and stealth of days! 'tis now
    Since thou art gone,
Twelve hundred hours, and not a brow
    But clouds hang on.
As he that in some cave's thick damp
    Locked from the light,
Fixeth a solitary lamp,
    To brave the night
And walking from his sun, when past
    That glimmering ray
Cuts through the heavy mists in haste
    Back to his day,
So o'er fled minutes I retreat
    Unto that hour
Which showed thee last, but did defeat
    Thy light, and power,
I search, and rack my soul to see
    Those beams again,
But nothing but the snuff to me
    Appeareth plain;
That dark, and dead sleeps in its known,
    And common urn,
But those fled to their Maker's throne,
    There shine, and burn;
O could I track them! but souls must
    Track one the other,
And now the spirit, not the dust
    Must be thy brother.
Yet I have one *pearl* by whose light
    All things I see,
And in the heart of earth, and night
    Find Heaven, and thee.

If the 'twelve hundred hours' are taken literally, then this elegy for William Vaughan was written very early in September 1648, since his death occurred about 14 July. The poet returns in memory to the 'hour' when he watched at the bedside as his brother died, but since William's light has been extinguished like a candle, all that is left is the 'snuff' – the material body, which is 'dark, and dead' – while his soul has returned to its Maker, where it continues to 'shine, and burn'. The poet longs to 'track' his brother and other lost loved ones, but he has to face the fact that only a soul can follow another soul to heaven and all that is left of William on earth is the 'dust' that has been consigned to the 'common urn' of the grave. His consolation in the last four lines is that he still has the light that shines from the 'pearl' of the Bible by which he knows that he will one day find heaven and be reunited with William.

The Constellation

Fair, ordered lights (whose motion without noise
    Resembles those true joys
Whose spring is on that hill where you do grow
    And we here taste sometimes below,)

With what exact obedience do you move
    Now beneath, and now above,
And in your vast progressions overlook
    The darkest night, and closest nook!

Some nights I see you in the gladsome east,
    Some others near the west,
And when I cannot see, yet do you shine
    And beat about your endless line.

Silence, and light, and watchfulness with you
    Attend and wind the clue,[1]
No sleep, nor sloth assails you, but poor man
    Still either sleeps, or slips his span.[2]

He gropes beneath here, and with restless care
    First makes, then hugs a snare,
Adores dead dust, sets heart on corn and grass
    But seldom doth make heaven his glass.

Music and mirth (if there be music here)
    Take up, and tune his year,
These things are kin to him, and must be had,
    Who kneels, or sighs a life is mad.[3]

Perhaps some nights he'll watch with you, and peep
        When it were best to sleep,
Dares know effects,[4] and judge them long before,
        When the herb he treads knows much, much more.

But seeks he your *Obedience, Order, Light,*
        Your calm and well-trained flight,
Where, though the glory differ in each star,
        Yet is there peace still, and no war?

Since placed by him who calls you by your names
        And fixed there all your flames,
Without command you never acted aught
        And then you in your courses fought.

But here commissioned by a black self-will
        The sons the father kill,
The children chase the mother, and would heal
        The wounds they give, by crying, zeal.

Then cast her blood, and tears upon thy book[5]
        Where they for fashion look,
And like that lamb which had the dragon's voice[6]
        Seem mild, but are known by their noise.

Thus by our lusts disordered into wars
        Our guides prove wandering stars,
Which for these mists, and black days were reserved,
        What time we from our first love swerved.

Yet O for his sake who sits now by thee
        All crowned with victory,
So guide us through this darkness, that we may
        Be more and more in love with day:

Settle, and fix our hearts, that we may move
        In order, peace, and love,
And taught obedience by thy whole Creation,
        Become an humble, holy nation.

Give to thy spouse[7] her perfect, and pure dress,
        Beauty and *holiness,*
And so repair these rents, that men may see
        And say, *Where God is, all agree.*

[1] the thread that guides you. [2] wastes his life. [3] piety is madness. [4] natural causes. [5] the Bible. [6] a beast in the Book of Revelation. [7] the church as the bride of Christ.

Vaughan contrasts the obedience of stars as they move in order across the skies with the 'sloth', 'restless care', and pleasures ('music and mirth') that keep humankind from such watchful devotion to the Creator (stanzas 1-9). Peace maintained among the stars, even though they differ from each other in 'glory', is then set against war generated by 'black self-will' on earth (stanzas 10-12). The Civil Wars of the 1640s are described in traditional images – sons kill fathers, children pursue and butcher mothers – but this father is the king and this mother is the church, executed and dismantled by the 'zeal' of Puritans, who seek to justify their actions by appeal to the Bible. The last three stanzas pray for the peace and harmony of the constellations in a state that has been misled into 'mists' and 'darkness' and a church that has been ripped apart (stanzas 13-15). The one for whose sake this prayer is made, who 'now' sits in heaven 'crowned with victory', is primarily Christ (head of the universal church) but also Charles I (head of the Church of England).

They are all gone into the world of light!'

They are all gone into the world of light!
    And I alone sit ling'ring here;
Their very memory is fair and bright,
    And my sad thoughts doth clear.

It glows and glitters in my cloudy breast
    Like stars upon some gloomy grove,
Or those faint beams in which this hill is dressed,
    After the sun's remove.

I see them walking in an air of glory,
    Whose light doth trample[1] on my days:
My days, which are at best but dull and hoary,
    Mere glimmering and decays.

O holy hope! and high humility,
    High as the Heavens above!
These are your walks,[2] and you have showed them me
    To kindle my cold love,

Dear, beauteous death! the jewel of the just,
    Shining nowhere, but in the dark;
What mysteries do lie beyond thy dust;
    Could man outlook that mark![3]

He that hath found some fledged bird's nest, may know
    At first sight, if the bird be flown;
But what fair well, or grove he sings in now,
    That is to him unknown.

And yet, as Angels in some brighter dreams
    Call to the soul, when man doth sleep:
So some strange thoughts transcend our wonted[4] themes,
    And into glory peep.

If a star were confined into a tomb
    Her captive flames must needs burn there;
But when the hand that locked her up, gives room,
    She'll shine through all the sphere.

O Father of eternal life, and all
    Created glories under thee!
Resume thy spirit[5] from this world of thrall
    Into true liberty.

Either disperse these mists, which blot and fill
    My perspective[6] (still) as they pass,
Or else remove me hence unto that hill,
    Where I shall need no glass.[7]

[1] treat with contempt. [2] the walks of death. [3] the boundary of this world. [4] usual.
[5] the poet's soul, which belongs to God. [6] telescope. [7] artificial aid to sight.

In this elegy for William Vaughan, the third of the new poems added to the second edition of *Silex Scintillans* in 1655, there are signs of recovery from the deep despair of the earlier elegies through the healing agency of memory that can clear the poet's 'sad thoughts'. Vaughan can now accept death as 'the jewel of the just', which opens the way to the mystery of eternity where he imagines lost loved ones 'walking in an air of glory'. In the sixth stanza, the fledged bird that has flown the nest is an image of the soul that has left the body; and in the eighth, the soul (like a star in a tomb) is stifled by its imprisonment in the body but is able to shine in full glory when released by death. In the last two stanzas, Vaughan prays that God will either set him free entirely from 'this world' or clear away the mists that prevent him from gazing upon the 'glory' into which he can sometimes 'peep' (in stanza seven). He is now reconciled to whichever fate the Father has in store for him.

3
'Then keep the ancient way!':
Henry Vaughan and the Interregnum

Robert Wilcher

I

The personal grief experienced by Henry Vaughan at the deaths of a friend and a brother in 1648 – and the spiritual crisis it seems to have precipitated – can only have been deepened by the execution of the king on 30 January 1649 and the tightening of the new republic's grip on South Wales. During this time of turmoil, he occupied himself with translating poems from *The Consolation of Philosophy*, a Latin work from the early fifth century written by Severinus Boethius when he was in prison awaiting execution on a false charge of treason. These provided him with a means of venting his anger and distress by adapting the original texts to fit the circumstances of his own moment in history. One, for example, describes a human society in which the 'wicked', clearly identified as the victorious Puritans, have taken control:

> No perjuries, nor damned pretence
> Coloured with holy, lying sense
> Can them annoy, but when they mind
> To try their force, which most men find,
> They from the highest sway of things
> Can pull down great, and pious kings.

Another meditates on the power of Fortune to turn 'the state of things' upside down, overthrowing with 'headlong force the highest monarch's crown' and elevating into positions of authority the 'despised looks of some mechanic wretch'.

Early in 1649, the new regime set up two regional authorities in North and South Wales to levy collective fines for opposition to Parliament (known as 'delinquency') during the Second Civil War. At the start of 1650, these were replaced by a central committee in London, which nominated three subsidiary committees for North Wales, South Wales, and Monmouthshire. Of all the measures taken by the Council of State to ensure its control of church and state, however, the one that most affected the inhabitants of Breconshire was the Act for the Better Propagation and Preaching of the Gospel in Wales. One modern historian has argued that this Act constituted 'the real government of Wales' during the three years during which it was in force.[13] Another commentator describes the 'small cadre of ministers and laymen' in whom it invested power as 'almost manically industrious and peripatetic in the prosecution of their duties'.[14] Passed on 22 February 1650, the Act appointed commissioners who had the authority to examine local clergy and eject any who failed to conform to the Puritan standards of the regime, which included those who had supported the Royalist cause or resisted the ban on the *Book of Common Prayer* and traditional forms of worship. For example, when Henry's twin brother Thomas was formally evicted from Llansantffraed, one of the charges against him was that he had been 'in arms personally against the Parliament'; and Thomas Powell, one of Henry's closest friends, was found guilty of 'adhering to the King, and Reading Common Prayer'. Two hundred and seventy-five ejections took place across Wales, of which twenty-five were in Breconshire alone. Among those evicted from parishes in Vaughan's immediate neighbourhood, besides Powell from Cantref, was another of his friends, Thomas Lewes, rector of Llanfigan. Approvers, including Vavasour Powell and Walter Cradock, were appointed by Parliament to find suitable ministers to replace ejected clergy, or at least to supply regular itinerant preachers, but in the event every church within walking distance of Llansantffraed remained closed throughout most of the Interregnum period.

Llansantffraed Church, watercolour *c.*1884 (courtesy of Brecknock Museum)

Vaughan's personal state of mind at this time can be gauged from the introductory letter to the reader that he wrote on 17 April 1652 for a volume of prose translations that was eventually published under the title *Flores Solitudinis* (Flowers of Solitude) in 1654:

> All that may bee objected is, that I write unto thee out of a land of darknesse, out of that unfortunate region, where the Inhabitants sit in the shadow of death: where destruction passeth for propagation, and a thick black night for the glorious day-spring.

The general situation was so bad that the Six Counties of South Wales sent a petition to London in March 1652 pointing out that the people were enduring 'a Famine of the Word of God' and that 'the Churches are in most places shut up, and the Fabric thereof ready to fall to the ground for want of repair'. In these circumstances, some individuals defied their new masters. Powell and Lewes went on ministering to their parishioners as best they could; and the Revd Matthew Herbert – tutor to the Vaughan twins during the 1630s – who had been removed as rector of Llangattock as early as 1646, continued to preach to his flock until the county authorities put a stop to this illegal activity in 1655. He persisted in causing trouble, however, and was committed to Brecon jail for seventeen weeks in April 1656.

Alongside church commissioners and approvers, there were other local officials responsible for enforcing the observance of public fast days, suppressing

Llangattock village, sketch *c*.1830 (private collection)

sports and revels, detecting conspiracies and secret meetings, and preventing the expression of opinions antagonistic to the central government. As well as placing power in the hands of committed supporters like Jenkin Jones of Llandetty, who had been a captain in the Parliamentary army and became one of the most diligent and hated approvers in Vaughan's neighbourhood, the new regime also sought to engage former Royalists in the administration of the regions. Charles Walbeoffe was one of those who agreed to serve on various county committees in Breconshire. Although he held the office of High Sheriff, however, when the Second Civil War broke out in 1648 he promptly became a Commissioner of Array for the king. The following year, he had to face the charge that he 'sat as Justice of the peace in the court at Brecon when the friends of Parliament were prosecuted'. Nevertheless, he was once again employed in local government, until his support for the Six Counties Petition led to his removal from the Commission of the Peace in 1652. When he died a year later, Vaughan defended his integrity against those who had reviled him as a collaborator. In an elegy 'To the Pious Memory of C.W. Esquire', the poet expresses contempt for 'the public sorrow' displayed at the grand funeral of a man of considerable standing in his community and relates how he stole to the graveside later, an 'obscure mourner that would weep alone'. He explains that 'the might / Of love' has called him forth from his 'sad retirements' to become the 'just recorder' of his cousin's 'death and worth'. Some of the choices that Walbeoffe made during the 'tedious reign of our calamity' can be understood in the context of the 'storms and changes' of a time when 'none could see his way' clearly through the enveloping 'mists'. Throughout his career of public service, however, his 'just soul' had found ways of turning 'even hurtful things to good' and of mitigating the effects of 'bad laws'. Dismissing the errors of those who 'traduce' him for his engagement with the new political order of things, Vaughan manages to combine a defence of Walbeoffe's steadfast honesty with a stinging indictment of both central and local government under the victorious Puritans:

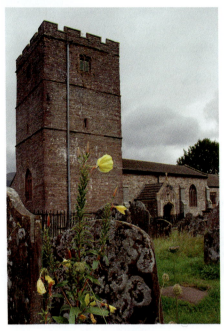

Llangattock Church

For though thy course in time's long progress fell
On a sad age, when war and opened hell
Licensed all arts and sects, and made it free
To thrive by fraud and blood and blasphemy:
Yet thou thy just inheritance didst by
No sacrilege, nor pillage multiply;
No rapine swelled thy state: no bribes, nor fees
Our new oppressors' best annuities.
Such clean, pure hands hadst thou!

II

The Interregnum saw various political changes as the 1650s wore on. The earlier republican arrangements were superseded in December 1653 by the Protectorate of Oliver Cromwell, whose religious views were more tolerant than those of many of his associates and subordinates. The hated Propagation Act had been allowed to lapse when it came up for renewal in March 1653 and the new Protector initiated policies that were less extreme than those of either the Nominated Parliament that sat from July to December 1653 or the 'propagators' on the ground in Wales. Soon after becoming Protector, he instituted a Board of Triers to examine the suitability of candidates for livings that had remained empty, with instructions to admit those who had not been convicted of acts of 'delinquency' against the Parliamentary cause. Nevertheless, no ministers were appointed to Llansantffraed, Llanfigan and Cantref, and the churches remained closed. The change of regime in London, however, did embolden some of Vaughan's neighbours to challenge the activities of Jenkin Jones, who had threatened Thomas Lewes, in a letter dated 31 January 1654, that he would

Llansantffraed Church, sketch *c.*1820 (courtesy National Library of Wales)

bring a troop of horse to break up his 'cock-fight' – the suspicion being that it was the cover for a secret meeting of Royalist sympathisers. A letter was sent to London in the hope of discrediting Jones with the new Protectorate authorities by claiming that he had no right to raise an armed force to 'terrify the country people'. This letter, which also complained about irregular proceedings by local justices of the peace, was dated from Newton on Ash Wednesday 1654 and signed by Thomas Vaughan, who must have been Henry's father (since his twin brother was then living in London). At the same time, Henry's friends, Thomas Powell and Thomas Lewes, together with another evicted clergyman, Griffith Hatley of Aberyscir, were engaged in heated correspondence with Jones about the prohibition on their preaching. There is no evidence that Henry Vaughan was involved directly in this political skirmish, but it is more than likely that his help would have been enlisted in drafting his father's mischievous attempt to incriminate Jenkin Jones and other Puritan officials in Brecon.

Henry Vaughan was certainly prepared to have his political colours pinned to the mast in some of the secular verse that was published in *Olor Iscanus* in 1651. Many of the poems in this volume had been written during the Civil Wars (such as his elegies on friends who died fighting for the king), but others were written after the regicide and the establishment of a republican government. One is an elegy for the fourteen-year-old princess Elizabeth, who had spent years in the custody of Puritan 'guardians' and never recovered from the trauma of her father's execution. After she died in Carisbrooke Castle on 8 September 1650, Vaughan wrote 'An Epitaph Upon the Lady Elizabeth, Second Daughter to His late Majesty', in which he makes a covert allusion to the execution of Charles I:

> Thy portion here was *grief*, thy years
> Distilled no other rain, but tears,
> Tears without noise, but (understood)
> As loud, and shrill as any blood.
> Thou seem'st a *rose-bud* born in *snow*,
> A flower of purpose sprung to bow
> To headless tempests, and the rage
> Of an incensed, stormy age.
> Others, ere their afflictions grow,
> Are timed, and seasoned for the blow,
> But thine, as *rheums*[1] the tenderest part,
> Fell on a *young* and *harmless* heart.

[1] watery discharge, such as tears or mucus.

The tears as 'shrill as any blood' are a reminder of the blood of King Charles I, which cries out for vengeance; and the reader who has 'understood' that allusion will readily pick up the significance of the 'headless' tempests that have swept across contemporary England. Others – older and more mature, like the young woman's own father – have been 'seasoned' like timber for the 'blow' of the axe; but she, who was forced to 'bow' to her captors as her father had to bow his head to the block, was '*young* and *harmless*'. Vaughan's subversive and carefully encoded message is that the Parliamentarians are not only guilty of murdering their political opponents; they also have the death of an innocent child on their consciences.

There were also opportunities for political commentary in the religious poetry to which Vaughan devoted his creative energies more and more exclusively after 1648. In 'Rules and Lessons', for example, along with instructions on how to conduct one's religious life throughout the day from waking to sleeping, the poet finds room for more subversive advice:

> To God, thy country, and thy friend be true,
> If *priest*, and *people* change, keep thou thy ground.
> Who sells *Religion*, is a *Judas Jew*,
> And, oaths once broke, the soul cannot be sound.

The true patriot and faithful Christian must hold firm to what Vaughan elsewhere calls 'the ancient way' and not follow the path of those who have betrayed king, country and church in the recent past. The first half of 'The Bird' is addressed to one of nature's innocent creatures whose nest has been buffeted by 'the busy wind all night' but who still greets the morning with 'early hymns' in praise of Providence for being clothed 'well and warm'; but the second half, in a series of discordant stanza forms, laments the condition of the human world in which the Prayer Book service of Matins has been banned and the only relief the oppressed can hope for is the return of Christ on the last day:

> But as these birds of light make a land glad,
> Chirping their solemn Matins on each tree:
> So in the shades of night some dark fowls be,
> Whose heavy notes make all that hear them, sad.
>
> The turtle then in Palm-trees mourns,
>   While owls and satyrs howl;
> The pleasant land to brimstone turns
>   And all her streams grow foul.[1]
>
> Brightness and mirth, and love and faith, all fly,
> Till the Day-spring[2] breaks forth again from high.

[1] the mourning turtle-dove, the owls and satyrs, and brimstone are all biblical images of political oppression and moral corruption. [2] a biblical image for Christ.

III

However determined Vaughan may have been to defend his dead cousin, Charles Walbeoffe, from the accusation of self-seeking collaboration, his own response to the blandishments of the new masters of church and state was quite different. That he was offered employment by the authorities in Brecon is evident from 'The Proffer', one of the most overtly political poems in the 1655 *Silex Scintillans*. The same occasion must have prompted a passage in 'The Importunate Fortune, Written to Doctor Powell of Cantref', a secular poem which is ostensibly a meditation on the baleful effects of the goddess of Fortune. The more personal and political significance of these lines would have been understood by the friend to whom they are addressed:

> For shame desist, why shouldst thou[1] seek my fall?
> It cannot make thee more monarchical.
> Leave off; thy Empire is already built;
> To ruin me were to enlarge thy guilt,
> Not thy prerogative.[2] I am not he
> Must be the measure to thy victory.
> The Fates hatch more for thee; 'twere a disgrace
> If in thy annals I should make a clause.[3]
> The future ages will disclose such men,
> Shall be the glory, and the end of them.

[1] Fortune or the Puritan regime. [2] area of special privilege or power. [3] a very small part.

The determination not to throw in his lot with an oppressive regime, as so many members of his local community had done, is expressed in the final stanza of his celebration of Pentecost, 'White Sunday', which invokes the example of an Old Testament figure who refused the bribe of a houseful of gold and silver to betray his people:

> O come! refine us with thy fire![1]
> Refine us! We are at a loss.
> Let not thy stars for *Balaam's* hire[2]
> Dissolve into the common dross!

[1] the tongues of flame that came down upon the Apostles on Whitsunday. [2] The story of the attempt to bribe Balaam is told in the Book of Numbers, chapter 22.

Vaughan, who confessed (in 'Misery') that he had a 'fierce soul', sometimes found it difficult to maintain the meekness and forgiveness demanded of him as a Christian. As early as 'The Mutiny', in the 1650 *Silex Scintillans*, he needed to check his desire to 'strive and struggle' against the foes of God – 'Not thine alone, but mine too', as he reminds his Maker and Judge; and late in the 1655 edition, he recalls that the blood of Abel was the first to cry out 'against a murderer' and wonders what divine punishment lies in store for the killers of his friends and his brother:

> What thunders shall those men arraign
> Who cannot count those they have slain,
> Who bathe not in a shallow flood,
> But in a deep, wide sea of blood?

Most of the time, however, he strove not to 'quarrel and grow bold' with God – to resist the impulse to 'travel, fight or die', as he puts in 'Misery'; and a poetic career that had begun at a time when the conflict between king and Parliament was starting to escalate toward civil war was effectively brought to a close in 'L'Envoy' on the last page of his great collection of religious verse with a prayer for national leaders to bring the trials and miseries of the past fifteen years to a peaceful end:

> Give watchful spirits to our guides!
> For sin (like water) hourly glides
> By each man's door, and quickly will
> Turn in, if not obstructed still.
> Therefore write in their hearts thy law,
> And let these long, sharp judgements awe
> Their very thoughts, that by their clear
> And holy lives, mercy may here
> Sit regent[1] yet, and blessings flow
> As fast, as persecutions now.
> So shall we know in war and peace
> Thy service to be our sole ease,
> With prostrate souls adoring thee,
> Who turned our sad captivity![2]

[1] with the implication of a restored monarchy. [2] a Biblical allusion to the bondage of the Israelites in Egypt or Babylon.

To my Worthy Friend, Master T. Lewes

> Sees not my friend, what a deep snow
> *Candies*[1] our country's woody brow?
> The yielding branch his load scarce bears
> Oppressed with snow, and *frozen tears*,
> While the *dumb* rivers slowly float,
> All bound up in an *icy coat*.

> Let us meet then! and while this world
> In wild *eccentrics* now is hurled,
> Keep we, like nature, the same *key*,
> And walk in our forefathers' way;
> Why any more cast we an eye
> On what *may come*, not what is *nigh*?
> Why vex our selves with *fear*, or *hope*
> And cares beyond our *horoscope*?
> Who into future times would peer
> Looks oft beyond his term set here,
> And cannot go into those grounds
> But through a *church-yard* which them bounds;
> Sorrows and sighs and searches spend
> And draw our bottom² to an end,
> But discreet joys lengthen the lease
> Without which life were a disease,
> And who this age a mourner goes,
> Doth with his tears but feed his foes.

¹ encrusts, as with sugar.   ² a skein of thread that is the length of our life.

This invitation to his friend and neighbour from across the Usk to visit him at a time when the river is frozen is typical of the resources with which Royalists saw out what has been called the 'Cavalier winter' of Puritan dominance. The first six lines, translated from an ode by the Roman poet Horace, are a subtle way of asserting cultural solidarity against their new political masters, who were mocked in Royalist propaganda for their lack of Latin and ignorance of classical literature; and there is a glance at the political situation of the friends in the word 'oppressed'. The summons to 'meet' and carry on the kind of civilised social intercourse known to their 'forefathers' is a way of coping with 'this world', which has been thrown off course by violent revolution. The advice to forget the fears and hopes prompted by horoscopes and be content with each day as it comes is also derived from Horace. After all, death lies in store for everyone and a future beyond the grave is reached only 'through a *church-yard*'. The 'term' of each person's existence is already fixed, and 'sorrows and sighs' only make the thread of life run out more quickly. But the 'discreet joys' that good companions can share quietly together render our allotted span here worthwhile even in times of political persecution. Besides, in 'this age' we must avoid giving satisfaction to our 'foes' by letting them see our distress. This is a fine example of the secular poetry that Vaughan continued to write during the Interregnum, when his main poetic energies were going into the religious verse of *Silex Scintillans*.

The Proffer

Be still, black parasites,
  Flutter no more;
Were it still winter, as it was before,
  You'd make no flights;
But now the dew and sun have warmed my bowers,
  You fly and flock to suck the flowers.

  But you would honey make:
    These buds will wither,
And what you now extract, in harder weather
    Will serve to take;[1]
Wise husbands[2] will (you say) their wants prevent,[3]
  Who do not so, too late repent.

    O poisonous, subtle fowls!
      The flies of hell
That buzz in every ear, and blow on souls
      Until they smell
And rot, descend not here, nor think to stay,
  I've read, who 'twas, drove you away.

    Think you these longing eyes,
      Though sick and spent,
And almost famished, ever will consent
      To leave those skies,
That glass of souls and spirits, where well dressed
  They shine in white (like stars) and rest.

    Shall my short hour, my inch,
      My one poor sand,[4]
And crumb of life, now ready to disband
      Revolt and flinch,
And having borne the burden all the day,
  Now cast at night my Crown away?

    No, no; I am not he,
      Go seek elsewhere.
I skill not[5] your fine tinsel, and false hair,
      Your sorcery
And smooth seducements: I'll not stuff my story
  With your Commonwealth and glory.

    There are, that will sow tares
      And scatter death
Amongst the quick,[6] selling their souls and breath
      For any wares;

> But when thy Master comes, they'll find and see
> There's a reward for them and thee.
>
> Then keep the ancient way!
> Spit out their phlegm
> And fill thy breast with home; think on thy dream:
> A calm, bright day!
> A land of flowers and spices! the word given
> *If these be fair, O what is Heaven!*

¹ will do to eat. ² husbandmen. ³ anticipate. ⁴ in an hour glass that measures his life. ⁵ do not care for. ⁶ the living.

This poem from the 1655 *Silex Scintillans* is Vaughan's contemptuous response to the offer of a place in local administration during the Interregnum. The 'black parasites', 'subtle fowls' and 'flies of hell' are agents of the Puritan state, who tempt former supporters of the king to collaborate with the new regime and who have approached the poet at a time when he is recovering from the Civil Wars, perhaps from ill health or perhaps from economic difficulties – his 'bowers' once again being warmed by the 'sun'. The second stanza presents the arguments of the tempters: that if he wants to prove himself a 'wise' husbandman, he will make provision for the future now. In the third stanza, he rejects these tempters as devils ('flies of hell') whose breath corrupts and reminds them that God drove away the plague of flies from Egypt.

The next two stanzas indignantly reject the proposal that after suffering persecution for so long he should turn his eyes away from the 'skies' (where those who died for the king now 'shine in white') and 'revolt and flinch' in his own loyalty. He insists that if he is nearing the end of his days (his 'crumb of life' being about to 'disband'), he will not forfeit his 'Crown' – either his devotion to the Royalist cause or the reward of immortality promised to the true Christian – for the merely material prosperity being offered. In the sixth stanza, he declares that he has no interest in the baits held out to him (which are nothing more than 'tinsel' and 'false hair') and scornfully dismisses all attempts to add to the glory of the Commonwealth by becoming part of the ignominious 'story' of collaboration. The next stanza alludes to the parable of the weeds ('tares') sowed by the devil, which will be cast into the fires of hell – the ironic 'reward' that awaits his Puritan tempters and those who sell their souls to them, when Christ ('thy Master') comes to judge the world. This angry and defiant poem ends with an appeal to other Royalists who may be tempted to throw in their lot with the enemy. If they remain steadfast to the 'ancient way' of monarchy and religion, they will be truly rewarded with a heavenly 'home' that will be even better than their 'dream' of peace and prosperity on earth.

The Men of War

Luke: Chapter 23, verse 11
[And Herod and his men of war set him at nought, and mocked him, and arrayed him in a gorgeous robe, and sent him again to Pilate.]

If any have an ear
Saith holy John, then let him hear.
He that into captivity
Leads others, shall a captive be.
Who with the sword doth others kill,
A sword shall his blood likewise spill.
Here is the patience of the saints,
And the true faith, which never faints.[1]
Were not thy word (dear Lord!) my light,
How would I run to endless night,
And persecuting thee and thine,
Enact for *saints*[2] my self and mine.
But now enlightened thus by thee,
I dare not think such villainy;
Nor for a temporal self-end
Successful wickedness[3] commend.
For in this bright, instructing verse[4]
Thy saints are not the conquerors;
But patient, meek, and overcome
Like thee, when set at naught and dumb.
Armies thou hast in Heaven, which fight,
And follow thee all clothed in white,
But here on earth (though thou hast need)
Thou wouldst no legions, but wouldst bleed.
The sword wherewith thou dost command
Is in thy mouth, not in thy hand,
And all thy saints do overcome
By thy blood, and their martyrdom.
But seeing soldiers long ago
Did spit on thee, and smote thee too;
Crowned thee with thorns, and bowed the knee,
But in contempt, as still we see,
I'll marvel not at aught they do,
Because they used my Saviour so;[5]
Since of my *Lord* they had their will,
The servant must not take it ill.
　Dear *Jesus* give me patience here,
And faith to see my Crown[6] as near
And almost reached, because 'tis sure
If I hold fast and slight the *lure*.[7]

Give me humility and peace,
Contented thoughts, innoxious[8] ease,
A sweet, revengeless, quiet mind,
And to my greatest haters kind.
Give me, my God! a heart as mild
And plain, as when I was a child;
That when *thy Throne is set*, and all
These *conquerors*[9] before it fall,
I may be found (preserved by thee)
Amongst that chosen company,
Who by no blood (here) overcame
But the blood of the *blessed Lamb*.[10]

[1] Vaughan paraphrases this passage from the Book of Revelation, Chapter 13, verses 9 and 10. [2] Vaughan was contemptuous of the way the Puritans adopted the title of 'saints'. [3] like that of the victorious Puritans. [4] the verse from Luke's gospel. [5] Parliamentary soldiers are like the Roman legionaries who mocked Christ long ago. [6] the crown of immortal life. [7] resist the temptation to collaborate. [8] harmless. [9] the victorious Puritan armies. [10] the blood shed by Christ on the Cross.

This is one of Vaughan's clearest statements of his desire to follow the Christian doctrine of meeting provocation with meekness and wrongs with forgiveness. He admits that if he followed his natural inclination, he would 'run to endless night' and be no better than those who style themselves 'saints'. But the light of the Gospel has shown him another path and he knows that the true saints are not those who glory in conquest. His model is Christ, who faced the abuse and mockery that preceded his crucifixion with patience and humility, and as his 'servant' he must do likewise. His consolation for enduring 'successful wickedness' in this life without seeking revenge is the prophecy of St John that everyone – the 'conquerors' and the 'chosen company' of the saved – will come before the throne of God for judgement.

4

'Then bless thy secret growth': Henry Vaughan and the Church

Helen Wilcox

I

Most great literature is concerned in some way with love and loss. In the case of Henry Vaughan, his writings demonstrate an overriding love of God and a passionate devotion to the natural world, particularly his native Usk Valley in South Wales. These two loves are inseparable since, in Vaughan's perception, the creation is filled with the immanence of its creator. The poetry is also frequently elegiac in tone, deeply affected by the death of his beloved younger brother William in 1648 and the loss of his first wife Catherine in the early 1650s, which gave rise to some of his most moving verse. In addition, however, one of the most important factors in Vaughan's life and work was the loving and losing of a rather different object of affection – not a person, a landscape or even faith itself, but an institution, the church.

Vaughan grew up under what he felt to be the benevolent influence of the Church of England – or as he preferred to call it, 'The British Church' – which had been established in the Elizabethan era of the previous century. In his prose work *The Praise and Happinesse of the Countrie-Life* (1651), Vaughan describes the 'pious and beautifull work' of a parish church – like those he had worshipped in as a boy at Llansantffraed and Llangattock – on a festival day:

> The *doore-keepers* of the *house* of *God* set wide open their *beautifull gates*. The *Church-bels* Ring, and every pious Soule is ravish'd with the *Musick*, and is sick of love untill he come into the *Courts* of the *Lord*. The *Temples* and *Communion tables* are drest, and the *beauty of holinesse* shines everywhere.

The language used by Vaughan in this evocative account (a loose translation of a Spanish original) is not only biblical, echoing the *Song of Songs* with the phrase 'sick [as a result] of love', but also sensuous, expressing the churchgoers' longing for their eyes and ears to be 'ravish'd'. The church offers Vaughan both aesthetic delight and spiritual nourishment: it is a physical building, adorned with the beauty befitting the 'house of God', and at the same time it is the metaphysical setting for an encounter with 'holinesse'.

Vaughan's love of the church went far beyond affection for a particular place or style of worship, fundamental though that clearly was to his own experience. The church signifies for Vaughan a divinely ordained leadership and authority in spiritual matters, the familiar order and cycle of the liturgical year with its seasons and festivals, the daily and weekly pattern of worship and bible-reading according to the liturgy and lectionary laid down in *The Book of Common Prayer*, and a rule of life for private devotion inspired by shared ideals of prayer and obedience. This communal function of the church, even in terms of personal piety, is vital: indeed, the church is not so much a place as a communion or coming together of people. Vaughan's understanding of the church is based on two key biblical metaphors of community, one of which (as may be seen in his poems 'The World (I)' and 'The Search') depicts the church as the bride of Christ, an image suggesting that faith leads to a loving partnership with the saviour himself. The second of these metaphors originates in the biblical account of the church as the body of Christ (St Paul's definition in I Corinthians 12: 27), suggesting therefore that all individual believers are 'members' of the one body in a state of mutual dependence. It is thus quite apt for us to regard Vaughan's attitude to the church as love: not only did he delight in everything that it signified liturgically and aesthetically in his daily life and spiritual practice, but it enabled him to experience a sense of relationship with fellow 'members' of the 'body' as well as with Christ himself.

II

It is vital for us to understand the enormous significance of the church to Vaughan, in order that we may fully appreciate the profound loss that he suffered when this institution as he knew it was taken from him. In the mid-seventeenth century, ecclesiastical loyalties were inevitably bound up with political allegiances, and Vaughan was no exception to this; as a keen Royalist, he played his part in defending all that Charles I stood for, including the established church, by fighting in the Civil War in Cheshire in 1645 (see Chapter Two). Since the king was by law the head of the church, the eventual success of the Parliamentary army against the Royalist forces spelled disaster for the church. In 1645, *The Book of Common Prayer* was banned by Parliament: the order stated that this mainstay of church liturgy 'shall not remain, or be from henceforth used in any Church, Chappel, or place of publique Worship, within the Kingdome of England, or Dominion of Wales'. The Prayer Book was to be replaced by the Puritan *Directory for the Publique Worship of God*, which challenged the role of sacred locations, and church buildings in particular, by pronouncing that 'no place is capable of any holiness under pretence of whatsoever Dedication or Consecration'. In 1646, Vaughan's schoolmaster, Matthew Herbert, was removed from Llangattock and replaced by a Puritan minister. In 1650, the Act for the Better Propagation and Preaching of the Gospel in Wales led to the further eviction of more than a dozen priests from their livings in the Usk Valley alone, including Vaughan's own brother Thomas from Llansantffraed (see Chapter Three). The Act was implemented with revolutionary gusto in South Wales, where according to Peter Thomas nearly two hundred clergy were expelled and not replaced, and 'the faithful orthodox' found themselves 'unceremoniously cast out into the wilderness'.[15] The lively churches of the immediate past, along with their priests, liturgy and community, were forcibly removed from Vaughan's life. Like many others at the time, he lost that crucial aspect of his identity, both social and spiritual, which was bound up with the church.

The effect on Vaughan was comparable to bereavement, and his writing betrays a kind of disorientation similar to that resulting from the separation of lovers. Dismay and anger at this loss of the church can be heard throughout his volume of poems, *Silex Scintillans* (1650, 1655), as we shall see, while his 1652 prose work, *The Mount of Olives*, tellingly includes '*A prayer in time of persecution and Heresie*' in which God, 'the Prince of peace', is asked to heal 'these present sad breaches and distractions':

> Consider, O Lord, the teares of thy Spouse which are daily upon her cheeks, whose adversaries are grown mighty, and her enemies prosper. The wayes of *Zion* do mourne, our beautiful gates are shut up, and the Comforter that should relieve our souls is gone far from us. Thy Service and thy Sabbaths, thy own sacred Institutions and the pledges of thy love are denied unto us.

The 'beautiful gates' – noticeably, the same phrase that Vaughan used in his celebration of the church's shining glory, when the gates were 'set wide open' to welcome the festival day – are now firmly and coldly 'shut up'. The relationship between God and his 'Spouse' the church has turned from joyous marriage to sorrowful mourning, and 'the pledges of [God's] love' in the liturgy and Holy Communion have disappeared.

A similar language of exclusion is found in the Latin poem prefacing his 1651 collection, *Olor Iscanus*. Vaughan addresses the poem to 'Posterity' and (in Alan Rudrum's translation) speaks of the 'harsh' times through which he lived:

I lived at a time when religious schism had divided and fragmented the English people, amongst the furies of priest and populace. When these afflictions first raged through our pleasant land, a vile weed cast down the sacred rose, and the fountains were muddied; peace was drowned in the troubled waters, and a gloomy shadow overcast the days of splendour.[16]

The 'sacred rose' cast down in favour of a 'vile weed' refers both to the late king and to the church, the biblical 'Rose of Sharon', which has been stripped of all its 'splendour'. The church, the body of Christ, has been scattered, and its dislocated and dispersed members face exile. Vaughan's writing takes on a new vocabulary of suffering, including, here, violent affliction, gloomy shadows and the muddied waters of what should be the church's pure fountain – and, in subsequent texts, the wilderness of exile. In the dedication of *The Mount of Olives*, Vaughan writes that he aims to '*commiserate* distressed Religion', comparing the current situation of the church to that of a '*wayfaring*' pilgrim in '*a weary land*' or '*waste and howling Wildernesse*'. In his poem 'The Bee', Vaughan talks of truth being 'trodden down, and spoiled' like soiled snow, and religion itself being 'Exiled'. His dual sense of loss – losing the church, and losing his way in the resultant wilderness – is all the more painful since it occurs in his own home country, not in some far distant land. His experience of what Philip West calls 'internal exile' is doubly disorienting.[17]

Llansantffraed Church, a watercolour by John Swete *c.*1792
(courtesy National Library of Wales)

Vaughan's distress at the fate of the church is given its most intense expression in his short lyric from the first part of *Silex Scintillans*, entitled 'The British Church'. For readers at the time, his choice of title would have immediately called to mind the poem of the same title by George Herbert, the devotional poet whose work was very widely read in the mid-seventeenth century and greatly influenced Vaughan's turn to religious lyrics. In Herbert's poem, published in 1633, 'The British Church' is joyfully celebrated as a 'deare Mother' who is 'Neither too mean, nor yet too gay': she has found the ideal middle way between the 'painted' Catholic church 'on the hills' of Rome and 'She in the valley', the Calvinist church of Geneva, who is 'so shie / Of dressing' that she 'nothing wears'. In Vaughan's poem, by contrast, there is no possibility of praise for the church. In fact, it is the church who speaks, and she is in distress:

> Ah! he is fled!
> And while these here their *mists*, and *shadows* hatch,
> My glorious head
> Doth on those hills of myrrh, and incense watch.

Vaughan's own sense of having been abandoned is mirrored in the voice of the church as she exclaims that the Lord, her 'glorious head', has gone away to the perfumed hills of heaven, leaving her alone amid the 'mists, and shadows' of the Puritans who (in Vaughan's view) obscure the clear light of truth. The

Llansantffraed Church interior (photograph by Hywel Bevan)

poem's devastating biblical echoes suggest that these enemies of the church are more evil than the soldiers who crucified Christ and cast lots for his clothes at the foot of the cross:

> Haste, haste my dear,
> The soldiers here
> Cast in their lots again,
> That seamless coat
> The Jews touched not,
> These dare divide, and stain.

In the religious turmoil of 1650s Britain, those who oppose the established church are prepared to 'divide' the 'seamless coat' left intact on the first Good Friday – a metaphor for Christ's body, the undivided church, now torn apart by dissent and division.

In the second stanza of the poem, Vaughan sets up a disturbing half-echo of the soul 'ravish'd' by church music in Vaughan's description of former days: by 1650, the church has 'ravish'd looks', applying the same adjective but with a fiercely negative and sexualised meaning. The contrast with Herbert's personified 'British Church' is striking; she was not vulnerable to attack and was serenely able to show the world her 'fine aspect in fit array'. No wonder Vaughan's church, by contrast, calls plaintively on her 'dear' spouse to return quickly and resurrect her 'slain flock'. As the poem ends, she once again urges Christ to move as swiftly 'As a young roe / Upon the mounts of spices'. Even in

Llansantffraed Church

his awareness of the desperate situation of the church, Vaughan could combine biblical imagery (again, here, from the *Song of Songs*) with visionary and sensual immediacy, arresting the reader's attention with palpable effect. To drive home his point with final intensity, Vaughan assembles a series of biblical allusions to form a closing epigraph in Latin, in which the 'rose of the field', the church herself, is described as having been made into 'food for swine'.

III

One of the ironies of Vaughan's life is that he wrote his best poetry in a concentrated period, approximately 1648-1655, which was precisely the time when he lost his brother, his first wife, the Civil War, the king, and the church. Out of multiple griefs came the motivation to write and, in the absence of the accustomed support of the church, it was Vaughan's writing which enabled him to rediscover, or recreate, the church in new and perhaps unexpected places. As Louis Martz remarked, 'it is as though the earthly church had vanished, and man were left to work alone with God'.[18] This holy 'work' led Vaughan to a variety of textual strategies for dealing with the 'vanished' church, three of which I wish to explore in the remainder of this chapter.

The first compensatory spiritual activity for Vaughan was, as the discussion of 'The British Church' has already suggested, to engage in an extended poetic conversation with George Herbert. This takes the form of innumerable allusions to Herbert's poems in Vaughan's own, but it also consists of reworkings of Herbert's poems in Vaughan's distinctive manner and for the needs of his own generation. In the preface to *Silex Scintillans* (1655), Vaughan announces to his readers that the great inspiration behind his devotional poems was the 'holy *life* and *verse*' of 'the blessed man, Mr *George Herbert*'. Vaughan (rightly) noted that he was not alone in being so influenced by Herbert, whose work 'gained many pious *converts*, (of whom I am the least)'. The reasons for this were not only Herbert's evident skills in rhetoric and lyric poetry but the fact that he wrote, with confident affection, about the flourishing church before the Civil War, as we have seen in comparing his poem 'The British Church' with Vaughan's. Herbert's 1633 volume of poems was posthumously published under the title *The Temple* – a term that, by the 1650s, had become an evocative shorthand for the outlawed church – and the three sub-sections are entitled, respectively, 'The Church-porch', 'The Church' and 'The Church Militant'. Even more significant to Vaughan than these resonant connections with the pre-Civil War church, however, was the fact that the earlier poet set an example to subsequent writers by aiming not so much at '*verse*' as at spiritual '*perfection*' by means of his poetry. Vaughan admired Herbert because he wrote from 'true, practic piety' and sought to nourish the devotional zeal of his readers. This, I would suggest, is what Vaughan was attempting to achieve for himself and his readers with *Silex Scintillans*. In choosing to call the contents of his collection 'hymns', Vaughan was deliberately echoing Herbert's poem 'A true Hymne', where genuine religious lyrics are defined as the poems in which 'the soul unto the lines accords' and a spiritual impulse guides the poet's pen.

Vaughan's poems, therefore, have a pastoral purpose: they set about reconstructing and reinvigorating some fundamental aspects of the church's 'ancient way' (as he refers to it in 'The Proffer') to which he and his contemporaries have, in the 1650s, been denied access. Like Herbert, Vaughan writes poems associated with festivals from the liturgical year – *Silex Scintillans* contains lyrics entitled 'Christ's Nativity', 'Palm-Sunday', 'Easter-Day', 'Ascension-Day', 'White Sunday', 'Trinity-Sunday' – in order to keep alive the patterns of the church's year which are otherwise obliterated by the Puritan abolition of Christmas and other traditional celebrations. This is an issue taken up explicitly in the second set of verses under the title 'Christ's Nativity'. Vaughan's poems include 'Church Service' which, as in Herbert's 'Antiphon' poems, recreates the experience of participating in church music in order to worship 'the God of harmony, and love!' Vaughan and his readers may not be able to meet and sing together in a church, but in the lines of his poem they can 'stand' in a 'choir of souls'. In his poem 'Son-days', he takes delight in the special day on which the believer experiences 'Heaven once a week'. The language and sentiments are very close to Herbert's in his poem 'Sunday', but Vaughan's lyric is even closer to the technique of Herbert's poem 'Prayer (I)' in which a sequence of descriptive phrases suggest that prayer is a reciprocal process by which heaven and earth seem to change places. Vaughan's vision of Sunday is remarkably similar:

> The creatures' Jubilee; God's parle with dust;
> Heaven here; man on those hills of myrrh, and flowers;
> Angels descending; the returns of trust;
> A gleam of glory, after six-days-showers.

The closeness to Herbert's mood, technique and spirituality in these lines is striking and would undoubtedly have been an important part of Vaughan's readers' rediscovery of the 'ancient' Church on the printed page. They would also have recalled the opening line of the poem consciously evoked in 'Son-days', Herbert's 'Prayer (I)', which begins: 'Prayer, the Churches banquet'. What Vaughan is celebrating, indirectly by means of his reference to Herbert's poetic collection, is the communal prayer of Sundays, the liturgical worship of the church gathered together for the Eucharistic 'banquet'.

In the absence of the church and its regular Prayer Book services, Vaughan thus brings an alternative liturgy into being through his poems. In 'Dressing', he asks God to give him 'mystical *Communion*' when the material sacrament is missing through the closure of the churches. In 'Holy Scriptures', he praises the power of the Bible to express 'The Word in characters' and transpose God into 'the voice' as would otherwise have taken place in the liturgical readings from scripture. Further, in his prose work *The Mount of Olives*, Vaughan makes available a set of prayers and meditations which constitute a kind of substitute for the banned *Book of Common Prayer*. The subtitle, 'Solitary Devotions', is particularly telling and connects with the comment in Vaughan's dedicatory epistle that, since Jesus had 'no place to put his head in' but 'took up his *nights-lodging* in the cold *Mount of Olives*', his 'Servants' in post-Civil War Britain 'must not think the *present measure* too hard'. The reference in '*present measure*' to the situation in Wales, where the Act for the eviction of clergy and closure of churches was so stringently enforced, is unmistakable. Defiantly, Vaughan notes in *The Mount of Olives* that the 'reverend and sacred buildings' which are 'now vilified and shut up' will for him always be 'solemn and publike places of meeting' for worship and sacraments; and, because of the presence of God in them, 'that *Ground is holy*'.

IV

In contrast to this almost nostalgic sense that there is a special holiness associated with a church building, Vaughan also asserts in *The Mount of Olives* that God is 'every where'. In this paradox we may begin to discern the second of Vaughan's strategies to compensate for the loss of the church. One of his elegiac poems begins 'I walked the other day (to spend my hour)', an opening line which tells of an alternative place for the conventional hour of prayer and worship – the outdoors, through which he walks daily. As Jonathan Nauman demonstrates in Chapter Five, Vaughan is one of the most passionate poetic observers of the natural world, but the reason for this is the profound sense, as expressed in 'I walked the other day', that God is present 'in all things', in every aspect of the creation, 'though invisibly'. Vaughan's poems take particular delight in water, light, flowers, birds, earth and stars, but these and other aspects of nature are not praised for their own sake. Vaughan's purpose is that he and his readers may see 'in these masques and shadows' signs of God's 'sacred way'. To understand what eternity might mean, especially in the absence of the support normally offered by the liturgy and preachers in the church, Vaughan looks to the stars (in 'The World (I)') and the meadows (in 'The Retreat'), and begins to grasp the eternal metaphysical 'ring of light' and discern the first metaphorical 'bright shoots of everlastingness'. Spiritual wisdom comes from perceiving, in the eloquent phrase of critics Claude Summers and Ted-Larry Pebworth, a 'temple' in 'nature' itself.

Nowhere is this idea of a church in the natural world clearer than in Vaughan's poem 'The Morning-Watch'. Vaughan does not give this morning office of prayer the liturgical title 'Matins' (as Herbert did) but nonetheless stresses the ritual aspect of a 'watch' to mark the start of the day. The difference is that, instead of human voices singing psalms, the poem finds worship inherent in the 'great *chime* / And *symphony* of nature' itself:

> O joys! Infinite sweetness! with what flowers,
> And shoots of glory, my soul breaks, and buds!
>   All the long hours
>   Of night, and rest
>   Through the still shrouds
>   Of sleep, and clouds,
>   This dew fell on my breast;
>   O how it *bloods*,
> And *spirits* all my earth! hark! In what rings,
> And *hymning circulations* the quick world
>   Awakes, and sings ...

The sheer exuberance of the poem is typical of Vaughan in his almost unbounded delight in the song of nature. The natural world to Vaughan is constantly in motion, making the music of praise in '*hymning circulations*'. The effect is to infuse Vaughan's poetic language for his personal spiritual life with metaphors of natural growth: 'flowers', 'shoots' and – vitally, here used as a verb – 'buds'. The world is described as 'quick', suggesting its alert, energetic liveliness. As Jeremy Hooker has argued, 'quickness' is 'a formative word in [Vaughan's] incarnational vision'[19] (see also his commentary on this poem in Chapter One).

'The Morning-Watch', with its openness to the natural evidence of a new morning in creation, takes the place of the liturgy of Matins of which the poet has been deprived. Crucially, Vaughan's poem asserts that prayer is not primarily an activity of human beings walking *in* the natural world but is offered every morning *by* nature itself: 'Prayer is / The world in tune'. As the poem draws towards its conclusion, all is harmonious motion: the stars, though seemingly hidden by clouds, 'shine, and move / Beyond that misty shroud', while the prayerful songs of the birds join with those of human beings and set off an 'echo' in 'heaven's bliss'. The interconnectedness of heaven, nature and human experience is not only celebrated – it is in itself prayer, a new liturgy. In the final line of 'The Morning-Watch', the poet has found contentedness in knowing that, whether it is night or morning, both his 'lamp' and his 'life' will 'abide' in God's presence. Vaughan, at home in Wales yet in exile from the established church and its structures, learns this new mode of prayerfulness from the world around him in the Usk Valley: 'birds, beasts, all things /

Adore him in their kinds'. On the ground there are lessons to be found in the 'heraldry / Of stones, and speechless earth' ('Retirement (I)'), and above his head are the exemplary stars ('The Constellation') in their state of perfect devotion, characterised by 'Silence, and light, and watchfulness'.

V

Vaughan's hermetic understanding of nature led him to be especially interested in these implicit rather than explicit qualities of the creation, and in his fascination for the inner state of things lies what I suggest is the third and final way in which he re-establishes the church within his own spiritual life. If the buildings and practices of the institutional church are no longer available to the individual Christian, then an obvious response is to move inwards – to find, as Vaughan writes in his poem 'Dressing', the 'secret key' to open his 'desolate' inner rooms. If the 'ark' of the church (in the Old Testament imagery used by Vaughan in 'Jacob's Pillow, and Pillar') is to find its true home in these difficult times, then it will be in 'the meek heart' where 'the mild Dove doth dwell / When the proud waters rage'. The human heart may be a 'narrow pit', but Vaughan perceives that this is the place where God's 'holy flame' will 'lodge' until the church is released from its current 'captivity'. Vaughan also makes this view very clear in 'Religion': whereas in the time of Abraham heaven was very 'familiar' and it was quite common to see 'An Angel talking with a man', nowadays religion has retreated underground to its source in a 'secret, golden mine'. Spiritual strength,

View of hills near Llansantffraed (photograph by Philip Coyne)

of course, is to be found in this inwardness and secrecy. Donald Allchin suggests that there is something almost monastic in Vaughan's withdrawal, while Rowan Williams observes that Vaughan is repeatedly drawn to discover 'the hiddenness of the transcendent' and thereby to assert the mystery of God.

Not surprisingly, Vaughan's model for this hidden working of the spirit is nature itself, which sends seeds underground through the winter to prepare for new life and growth in the spring. My last poetic example, from which the title of this chapter is taken, is Vaughan's 'The Seed Growing Secretly'. The poem is based on the parable in St Mark's Gospel where Jesus likens the Kingdom of God to a seed which springs up as a plant, though the man who cast it into the ground has no idea how this has happened. Vaughan is evidently drawing a hopeful parallel between the seed and the British Church, cast down and yet mysteriously growing, preparing to 'spring and grow up' again, to the amazement of those who threw it away. The poet longs for the moment when he and the church will be able to 'spread and open' to God's will, but in the meantime he gives praise to God's uses of hiddenness. At the heart of Vaughan's poem is an address to the unseen life of the spirit:

> Dear, secret *greenness*! nursed below
> Tempests and winds, and winter-nights,
> Vex not, that but one sees thee grow,
> That One made all these lesser lights.

Llangorse Lake (photograph by Philip Coyne)

> If those bright joys he singly sheds
> On thee, were all met in one Crown,
> Both sun and stars would hide their heads;
> And moons, though full, would get them down.

Vaughan delights in this hidden 'greenness', the growing shoots of the young plant as it develops from the seed in secrecy, seen by God alone, the only one who matters. Like a metaphysical star shining in the darkness – a favourite image of Vaughan's – the hidden joys of the spirit are so bright that they would put the actual 'sun and stars' in the shade. The places of contentment and fruition, then, are the dark underground sites of waiting, and the 'narrow cell' of the bee in its hive, secretly creating the purest honey.

The poem's conclusion is to ask for a blessing on the 'secret growth' of the seed – the soul, the church – since it is a glorious thing to 'thrive unseen and dumb'. And thus it is possible to see that the loss of the church was perhaps for Vaughan a source of new spiritual life, as well as of the sorrow and anger that he so obviously expresses. As M. Wynn Thomas astutely comments, the paradox of the situation for Vaughan and other excluded churchgoers of his generation was that they were 'secretly blessed by historical catastrophe'.[20] Vaughan the writer certainly discovered three most fruitful textual modes of building an alternative church in exile: by writing a poetic liturgy inspired by the example of Herbert's *Temple*, by discovering a glorious 'temple' in nature itself, and by metaphorically retreating to narrow, dark, hidden spaces in order to grow and be blessed. Though he lived in an 'incensed, stormy age' (as he described it in 'An Epitaph upon the Lady Elizabeth'), Vaughan found a poetic voice to counter the persecution of his church and paradoxically discovered in his writing a new British Church.

The Morning-Watch

> O joys! Infinite sweetness! with what flowers,
> And shoots of glory, my soul breaks, and buds!
>   All the long hours
>   Of night, and rest
>   Through the still shrouds
>   Of sleep, and clouds,
>   This dew[1] fell on my breast;
>   O how it *bloods*,[2]
> And *spirits*[3] all my earth! hark! In what rings,
> And *hymning circulations* the quick world
>   Awakes, and sings;
>   The rising winds,
>   And falling springs,

>   Birds, beasts, all things
>   Adore him in their kinds.
>   Thus all is hurled
>   In sacred *hymns*, and *order*, the great *chime*
>   And *symphony*⁴ of nature. Prayer is
>   The world in tune,
>   A spirit-voice,
>   And vocal joys
>   Whose *echo* is heaven's bliss.
>   O let me climb⁵
>   When I lie down! The pious soul by night
>   Is like a clouded star, whose beams though said
>   To shed their light
>   Under some cloud,
>   Yet are above,
>   And shine, and move
>   Beyond that misty shroud.
>   So in my bed
>   That curtained grave, though sleep, like ashes, hide
>   My lamp, and life, both shall in thee⁶ abide.

¹ frequently a metaphor for divine grace. ² William Harvey had discovered the circulation of the blood in 1628. ³ in the old physiology, blood-begotten vital spirits animated the body. ⁴ harmony. ⁵ towards heaven in prayer. ⁶ in God.

An early photograph of Llansantffraed Church (courtesy Brecknock Museum)

In the first half of this poem, the joy of the poet, who is conscious of having received divine grace while he slept, modulates into the universal rejoicing of 'the quick world' at the break of a new day. The second half is a meditation on the nature and effects of prayer, which keeps the 'pious soul' safe in the hands of God even when it is shrouded in sleep. The alternation of long-lined and short-lined units of verse, making up nine sections in all, may be intended to reflect the *'chime / And symphony'* of the created world, since the universe was traditionally thought to consist of nine spheres, each emitting a musical note as it revolved, with all nine notes combining in perfect harmony.

The Seed Growing Secretly
Mark 4: 26

[And he said, So is the kingdom of God, as if
a man should cast seed into the ground.]

If this world's friends might see but once
What some poor man may often feel,
Glory, and gold, and crowns and thrones
They would soon quit and learn to kneel.

My dew, my dew![1] my early love,
My soul's bright food, thy absence kills!
Hover not long, eternal Dove![2]
Life without thee is loose and spills.

Something[3] I had, which long ago
Did learn to suck, and sip, and taste,
But now grown sickly, sad and slow,
Doth fret and wrangle, pine and waste.

O spread thy sacred wings and shake
One living drop! one drop life keeps!
If pious griefs Heaven's joys awake,
O fill his bottle![4] thy child weeps!

Slowly and sadly doth he grow,
And soon as left,[5] shrinks back to ill;
O feed that life, which makes him blow[6]
And spread and open to thy will.

For thy eternal, living wells
None stained or withered shall come near:
A fresh, immortal *green* there dwells,
And spotless *white* is all the wear.

Dear, secret greenness! nursed below
Tempests and winds, and winter-nights,

Vex not, that but one[7] sees thee grow,
That *One* made all these lesser lights.[8]

If those bright joys he singly sheds
On thee, were all met in one Crown,
Both sun and stars would hide their heads;
And moons, though full, would get them down.

Let glory be their bait,[9] whose minds
Are all too high for a low cell:
Though hawks can prey through storms and winds,
The poor bee in her hive must dwell.

Glory, the crowd's cheap tinsel still
To what most takes them, is a drudge;
And they too oft take good for ill,
And thriving vice for virtue judge.

What needs a conscience calm and bright
Within itself an outward test?
Who breaks his glass to take more light,
Makes way for storms into his rest.

Then bless thy secret growth, nor catch
At noise, but thrive unseen and dumb;
Keep clean, bear fruit, earn life and watch
Till the white winged Reapers[10] come!

The Priory Grove (photograph by Philip Coyne)

¹ the gift of life-giving grace. ² the Holy Spirit. ³ the speaker's first spiritual awakening, imagined as infancy. ⁴ a reference to Hagar's son, Ishmael, thirsting in the wilderness (Genesis 21: 14-19). ⁵ abandoned by God. ⁶ bloom. ⁷ only God. ⁸ stars and planets. ⁹ enticement. ¹⁰ the angels of the Apocalypse.

This poem contrasts the 'poor man' – likened to the 'poor bee' hibernating in its hive – with 'this world's friends', who seek a worldly 'glory' that is no more than 'the crowd's cheap tinsel'. Such a man knows that true 'life' is the gift of the Holy Spirit, which hovers over faithful souls and the community of the church, keeping their 'secret *greenness*' alive through times of persecution. He trusts that a 'fresh, immortal *green*', fed by the 'eternal, living wells' of God's grace, will survive the 'winter-nights' of oppression by the 'hawks' that 'prey through storms and winds'. As a private individual, member of an outlawed church, and defeated Royalist enduring the 'Cavalier winter', he knows that 'thriving vice' can be resisted by the 'secret growth' that thrives 'unseen and dumb' in the sure hope of ultimate victory.

Christ's Nativity (II)

How kind is heaven to man! If here
    One sinner doth amend
Straight there is joy, and every sphere¹
    In music doth contend;
And shall we then no voices lift?
    Are mercy, and salvation
Not worth our thanks? Is life a gift
    Of no more acceptation?
Shall he that did come down from thence,
    And here for us was slain,
Shall he be now cast off? no sense
    Of all his woes remain?
Can neither love, nor sufferings bind?
    Are we all stone, and earth?
Neither his bloody passions mind,²
    Nor one day bless his birth?
Alas, my God! Thy birth now here³
    Must not be numbered in the year.

¹ each of the nine spheres of the universe was believed to emit a note, all together making a perfect harmony. ² remember. ³ in a Britain currently ruled by Puritans.

This is the second of two sets of verses on the birth of Christ: the first calls upon the 'glad heart' to join the 'consort' of joy made by the natural world at the dawning of this special day in the liturgical calendar; this second poem laments that it is no longer possible to participate in the joyful music of the spheres in a state that has forbidden the celebration of Christmas as well as the solemn public remembrance of Christ's death on the Cross.

5
'The truth and light of things': Henry Vaughan and Nature

Jonathan Nauman

I

Henry Vaughan probably did not, in the earliest stages of his poetic career, anticipate becoming a literary figure especially associated with the world of nature and his native Usk Valley. His ambitions seem rather to have been directed toward the contemporary literary scene in Oxford and London, where he was attracted by friends and followers of Ben Jonson and Jonson's adopted protégé, Thomas Randolph. But his legal training in London was cut short by the outbreak of civil war in 1642, when he was recalled to Breconshire by his father.

Although the twenty-one-year-old poet seems not to have relished 'this enforced return to the pastoral landscapes of his boyhood',[21] his literary aspirations remained unblunted, and would also weather the failure in the mid-1640s of the Royalist cause, to which he himself, his family, and his closest friends were strongly loyal. Despite defeat and isolation from university and metropolitan culture, Vaughan continued for some time to envisage the possibility of preserving an afterglow of the literary world he had encountered as a student. From his country retreat in Breconshire, he addressed conventional love-poems to 'Amoret' and 'Etesia' and dreamed of joining an illustrious line of classicist poets, so that the River Usk would become as famous as Apollo's Eurotas, Orpheus's Hebrus, Petrarch's Tiber, Ausonius's Moselle, Sidney's Thames, and Habington's Severn. So long as a likeminded companion was available to sit with him by a roaring fire at a local inn and engage in real literary talk, he could leave 'the obtuse rout' of local money-grubbers 'to their husks' and scorn the 'black deeds' of the new Puritan masters of Brecon by subversively stealing 'a revel in the town' and enjoying 'a jest' at their expense. But this kind of heartiness and defensive roistering in his verse invitation to a 'Retired Friend' to visit him in 'Brecknock' (see Chapter Two) has a moral edge, which draws upon the parable of the Prodigal Son (who was reduced to eating 'husks' fed to pigs) and hints at desires deeper than his expressed need for conviviality and coterie wit.

Like many young men of his generation, Henry Vaughan even in his secular phase was – in Louise Guiney's words – 'deeply religious under a foam of worldliness'.[22] His English reading in the 1640s included not only the satires and love-poems of John Donne (1572-1631) and Thomas Randolph (1605-33), William Habington (1605-54) and Ben Jonson (1572-1637), but also the devotional poems of George Herbert (1593-1633); and as an accomplished Latinist, he not only translated works by the Roman poets Ovid and Juvenal but was also familiar with the songs and epistles of the fifth-century bishop, St Paulinus of Nola. In Vaughan's sacred verse, we find hints that the poet had promised God he would, in return for deliverance in bloody battle, dedicate his poetic talents to specifically Christian use; and he concluded a collection of verses from the Bible printed before his own poems in the 1655 *Silex Scintillans* with the following commitment: 'I will sacrifice unto thee with the voice of thanksgiving; I will pay that which I have vowed: salvation is of the Lord.' However, it took the war-related death of his younger brother to make Henry turn decisively to the visionary and devotional compositions for which he is now famous.

In his conversion and turn toward sacred verse, Vaughan would morally reject the enthusiastic pursuit of literary fame he had aspired to in his poem to the River Usk (see Chapter One). His new poetic vocation would seek intimations of 'a country / Far beyond the stars' ('Peace') and pursue transcendent helps and inward spiritual routes by which that country could be reached. Perhaps it is not surprising that one effect of this reorientation toward heavenly things was an increased clarity and intimacy in his gestures toward surrounding phenomena in nature. In his sacred phase, Vaughan became less inclined to subsume his Breconshire environs into classical literary ideals, and more inclined to let the natural world speak for itself as God's creation, as a book to help humanity unlearn sin.

II

Vaughan's sacred verses begin with the poem 'Regeneration', which depicts the poet's spiritual progress through a sequence of emblematic scenes, each providing an important but partial revelation, all leading to a moment of enlightenment and prayer to the Holy Spirit. The first stanza sets the scene, both external and inward:

> A ward,[1] and still in bonds, one day
>   I stole abroad,
> It was high-spring, and all the way
>   Primrosed, and hung with shade;
> Yet, was it frost within,
>   And surly winds
> Blasted my infant buds, and sin
>   Like clouds eclipsed my mind.
>
> [1] a minor under control of a guardian.

Vaughan initiates here a motif which will continue throughout his sacred verse, the allegory of man as a flower; and the dream-like sudden contrast, interweaving realistic descriptive setting with projected spiritual drama, gains especial conviction from the experiential tone of its natural detail. The process of projecting a spiritual condition on features of landscape and weather continues in the next stanza:

> Stormed thus, I straight perceived my spring
>   Mere stage, and show,
> My walk a monstrous, mountained thing
>   Rough-cast with rocks, and snow;
>   And as a pilgrim's eye
>   Far from relief,
> Measures the melancholy sky
>   Then drops, and rains for grief,
> So sighed I upwards still ...

Further on in the poem's journey, the speaker encounters a 'grove ... of stately height' that symbolizes the 'new spring' of Christ's revelation in the church.

Many of Vaughan's early non-devotional poems were occasional pieces, such as social invitations or commendations of other writers' work; and this literary inclination continued when he changed his subject to '*divine themes* and *celestial praise*'. Among what have come to be his most admired poems are a set of lyrics that appear to record visits to the graves of friends, and especially the burial place of his brother William. Vaughan had these poems printed without titles, but with a pilcrow or printer's paragraph mark (¶) placed above each of them. One of the best of these graveside meditations, the penultimate lyric of the first edition of *Silex Scintillans*, begins as if it were merely an account of a usual event:

> I walked the other day (to spend my hour)
>   Into a field
> Where I sometimes had seen the soil to yield
>   A gallant flower,
> But winter now had ruffled all the bower

> And curious store[1]
> I knew there heretofore.

[1] that is, the plants that flourished in the field during the summer.

The poet's 'hour' presents itself at first as a time of routine personal prayer during a walk in the winter countryside; but his ensuing contemplation gradually reveals that we are also witnessing a parable clarifying the spiritual import of William Vaughan's death:

> Yet I whose search loved not to peep and peer
> I'the face of things
> Thought with my self, there might be other springs
> Besides this here[1]
> Which, like cold friends, sees us but once a year,
> And so the flower
> Might have some other bower.[2]
>
> Then taking up what I could nearest spy
> I digged about
> That place where I had seen him to grow out,
> And by and by
> I saw the warm recluse[3] alone to lie
> Where fresh and green
> He lived of us unseen.

[1] that is, other seasons of spring in a realm beyond the earth. [2] the flower might still exist in another dimension. [3] the root.

The speaker's action, the digging in order to uncover the flower's root, is prefaced with an oblique suggestion that the reader (like the poet) should not merely 'peep and peer / I'the face of things', but look beneath the surface for spiritual meanings. And once the poet engages in dialogue with 'the warm recluse', it becomes clear that the actions he has recounted are intended to figure and express a Christian hope for bodily resurrection:

> Many a question intricate and rare
> Did I there strow,
> But all I could extort[1] was, that he now
> Did there repair
> Such losses as befell him in this air[2]
> And would ere long[3]
> Come forth most fair and young.

[1] get the root to admit. [2] that is, on earth. [3] in the spring (or, in William's case, at the Resurrection).

Most surprising of all is the sudden eruption of the subtext of human grief into the literal level of the poem:

> This passed, I threw the clothes quite o'er his head,
>   And stung with fear
> Of my own frailty dropped down many a tear
>   Upon his bed,
> Then sighing whispered, *Happy are the dead!*
>   *What peace doth now*
> *Rock him asleep below?*

In this stanza, metaphor and natural phenomenon seem to switch places, and the act of covering with bedclothes his dead brother's face in a paroxysm of mortal fear merges with the task of placing the soil back over the flower's root. And this eruption is not suppressed, for the whispered words that follow it seem to refer more appropriately to William's body than to the dormant flower: '*Happy are the dead! / What peace doth now / Rock him asleep below?*'

One might expect the poem at this juncture to complete the transition and directly reveal the poet's thoughts on the loss of his brother; but instead Vaughan pauses once again to consider the plant, pressing the point that the connection between the flower's root and the Christian doctrine of human resurrection is to be viewed not as fanciful, but as real:

> And yet, how few believe such doctrine springs
>   From a poor root

A path up a hillside near Llansantffraed (photograph Philip Coyne)

> Which all the winter sleeps here under foot
> And hath no wings
> To raise it to the truth and light of things,
> But is still trod
> By every wandering clod.

It is characteristic of Vaughan's response to the natural world that he should note how even humble creatures (like the 'poor root'), which are disregarded (trodden 'under foot') by heedless human beings, can teach spiritual lessons. And this consideration leads to a closing prayer which serves to clarify Vaughan's use of natural phenomena throughout *Silex Scintillans*:

> O thou![1] whose spirit did at first inflame
> And warm the dead,
> And by a sacred incubation fed
> With life this frame[2]
> Which once had neither being, form, nor name,
> Grant I may so
> Thy steps track here below,
>
> That in these masques and shadows I may see
> Thy sacred way,
> And by those hid ascents climb to that day
> Which breaks from thee[3]
> Who art in all things, though invisibly;
> Show me thy peace,
> Thy mercy, love, and ease,
>
> And from this care, where dreams and sorrows reign
> Lead me above
> Where light, joy, leisure, and true comforts move
> Without all pain,
> There, hid in thee, show me his life again
> At whose dumb urn
> Thus all the year I mourn.

[1] that is, God the Creator. [2] the body of the poet's brother. [3] the dawning of the eternal light of God.

The groves and flowers, waterfalls and wells of Vaughan's sacred verse are 'masques and shadows' that manifest God their Creator and lead the human observer towards him, but all are amplified rather than reduced, indeed paradoxically brightened and intensified, by the Spirit being present in them 'invisibly'. At its own level, the flower root thus derives from the same 'sacred incubation' that once informed with life the buried 'frame' of the poet's dead brother. The tracking of such 'hid ascents' indicates one of the major themes of the spirituality Vaughan intends his lyrics to communicate.

III

It is worth pausing to consider the terms 'sacred incubation' and 'hid ascents' more closely, since they are both related to Henry Vaughan's interest in hermetic or alchemical thought, a subject that his twin brother Thomas was avidly pursuing in Oxford and London during the time *Silex Scintillans* was being written. Henry shared Thomas's conviction that God's spiritual energies could be detected throughout his Creation through careful attention to certain physical phenomena and to human and animal (and vegetable and mineral) behaviour. In its approach to the physical world, hermetism led toward a vitalist understanding of the cosmos and away from the instrumental materialism that underlies most of current academic and scientific practice. Hermetic writings were avowedly experiment-centred, investigating how the material world actually functioned; but the hermetists' experiments were in practice heavily invested in neoplatonic and cabbalistic lore, presented in combination with the Judaeo-Christian scriptures. The opening sentences of one of Henry Vaughan's devotional treatises, 'Man in Darkness' (published in his prose volume, *The Mount of Olives*), gives some indication of the movement's tone and terminology, and also of its relevance to Vaughan's poetry:

> It is an observation of some *spirits*, that *the night is the mother of thoughts*. And I shall adde, that those thoughts are *Stars*, the *Scintillations* and *lightnings* of the soul strugling with *darknesse*. This *Antipathie* in her is *radical*, for being descended from the *house of light*, she hates a contrary *principle*, and being at that time a prisoner in some measure to an enemy, she becomes pensive, and full of thoughts. Two great *extremes* there are, which she equally abhors, *Darkness* and *Death*.

The human soul struggles at night, Vaughan says, because it takes its being or *'principle'* originally from God's abode in heaven, the supernatural *'house of light'* for which natural sunlight is a shadow or proxy. Night-time thoughts can thus be described as *'Stars'* or *'Scintillations'*, whose energies originally derive from heaven. (Visible stars in the sky, on the other hand, would be described in hermetic fashion as God's thoughts, actively mediating essential creative power to every animal, plant, and mineral on earth.) Even in the seventeenth century, Vaughan's technical hermetic vocabulary, characterizing God's Providence in terms of 'hid ascents' and God's creating as 'sacred incubation', would have seemed unusual and specialized; but as we have seen in 'I walked the other day', some of the poet's best devotional poems were strongly coloured by his imaginative embrace of this Christian-neoplatonic vision of the universe. Of all the poems in *Silex Scintillans*, 'Cock-crowing' is perhaps the most thoroughgoing in its use of hermetic terminology, one that also attains to the spiritual intensity that led Joseph H. Summers to describe Vaughan as 'a poet of astounding, if erratic, visionary and aural powers'.[23] In writing it, Vaughan may well have been thinking of his brother Thomas's alchemical treatises, and especially of a passage in *Anima Magica Abscondita* (1651), which contains many of the ideas addressed here:

> The *anima* [the world soul] though in some sense active, yet is she not so essentially, but a meer *Instrumentall Agent*, For she is guided in her Operations by a *Spirituall Metaphysical Graine*, a Seed or Glance of *Light*, simple and without any Mixture, descending from the *first Father of Lights*. For though his *full-ey'd* Love shines on nothing but *Man*, yet every thing in the World is in some measure directed for his Preservation by a *Spice* or *touch* of the *first Intellect*. This is partly confirmed by the Habitation and Residence of God: For he is seated *above all his Creatures*, to *hatch* as it were, and cherish them with *living Eternall Influences* which daily and hourely proceed from him.

'Cock-crowing' begins with an exclamation that is a Biblical term for God:

> Father of lights! what sunny seed,
> What glance of day hast thou confined
> Into this bird? To all the breed
> This busy ray thou hast assigned;
>   Their magnetism works all night,
>   And dreams of Paradise and light.
>
> Their eyes watch for the morning hue,[1]
> Their little grain expelling night
> So shines and sings, as if it knew
> The path unto the house of light.[2]
>   It seems their candle,[3] howe'r done
>   Was tinned[4] and lighted at the sun.

[1] colours of the dawn sky. [2] heaven, where the Father of Lights dwells.
[3] God-implanted instinct, like reason in man. [4] kindled.

The 'sunny seed', 'glance of day', 'busy ray', 'magnetism', and 'little grain' all refer to a supernatural mode of being in roosters, whereby they participate in the divine power that originally fashioned their species. Such hermetic imagery lends a technical immediacy that enlivens and galvanizes the poet's Christian meditation in response to the phenomenon of the bird that greets the dawn. Having composed his preliminary image of the rooster, Vaughan proceeds to consider the implications of its behaviour for his own situation as a human being made in the 'image' and 'likeness' of God (Genesis 1: 26-7):

> If such a tincture,[1] such a touch,
> So firm a longing can impower
> Shall thy own image think it much
> To watch for thy appearing hour?[2]
>   If a mere blast so fill the sail,
>   Shall not the breath of God prevail?

[1] an alchemical term for a spiritual principle infused into material things. [2] the time of Christ's return to earth to herald his eternal kingdom.

The creative actions of earthly nature, the solar light and heat that cause the instinctive crowing of the cock, have an 'immortal' counterpart discernible through human reason. In the next three stanzas, Vaughan acknowledges that a similar 'seed' to the creature's 'little grain' (that expels night in welcoming the sun) 'abides in' his own species, so that the human soul must strive to expel the darkness of bondage to sin and consciously pursue its own version of the bird's eager and energetic response to the dawn. He goes on to compare the faster beating of the rooster's 'pulse' at the return of sunlight with the human being's desire to fly towards the greater light of God. In the final stanzas of the poem, Vaughan addresses the main obstacle to his own soul's 'exalted flight' to heaven, namely his ailing physical body, for which he uses the biblical metaphor of a 'veil':

> Only this veil which thou hast broke,
> And must be broken yet in me,
> This veil, I say, is all the cloak
> And cloud which shadows thee from me.
>   This veil thy full-eyed love denies,
>   And only gleams and fractions spies.
>
> O take it off! make no delay,
> But brush me with thy light, that I
> May shine unto a perfect day,
> And warm me at thy glorious Eye!
>   O take it off! or till it flee,
>   Though with no lily, stay with me!

These final observations enable the poet to dream of 'Paradise and light' and to look forward to a time when his soul, released from the flesh, will experience not just 'gleams and fractions' of the warmth and light of the divine presence but the 'full-eyed love' of God.

IV

Many of Vaughan's attentions to nature and the landscape are similarly keyed toward encouraging human emulation. In some cases the advice is offered rather directly, as in the second stanza of 'Rules and Lessons':

> Walk with thy fellow creatures: note the *hush*
> And *whispers* amongst them. There's not a *spring*,
> Or *leaf* but hath his *morning-hymn*; each *bush*
> And *oak* doth know I AM;[1] canst thou not sing?

[1] the eternal creator and sustainer of life.

In other cases, such as the ecstatic opening of 'The Morning-Watch' – 'O joys! Infinite sweetness! With what flowers, / And shoots of glory, my soul breaks, and buds!' – and the pleas for spiritual watering in 'The Seed Growing Secretly' – 'My dew, my dew! my early love, / My soul's bright food' – an exemplary stream of consciousness is offered. Most often of all, as in 'Cock-Crowing', Vaughan calls attention to moral lessons implicit in the dependable behaviour of the creatures, especially in his longing for the humility and steadiness of the unselfconscious natural world in 'Distraction':

> Hadst thou
> Made me a star, a pearl, or a rain-bow,
> The beams I then had shot
> My light had lessened not,
> But now
> I find my self the less, the more I grow.

Elsewhere, he wishes his soul could shine with 'ardour' like the stars ('Midnight'), longs for the 'staidness' of birds and bees and flowers ('Man'), and vies with 'kind herbs' in sacred dutifulness ('The Favour'). The poet of *Silex Scintillans*, however, is not one to wander the Breconshire landscape romantically, 'lonely as a cloud'. God is always speaking through and in the creatures: 'by the beauty of the seat, / We plainly see, who made the same' ('Cock-crowing'). Nevertheless, there is a distinctive immediacy in Vaughan's invocation of natural phenomena that clearly implies particular and local observation. He remembers specific times from childhood in 'The Retreat': 'When on some *gilded cloud* or *flower* / My gazing soul would dwell an hour.' He hopes to be found as active 'as this restless, vocal *spring*' – evidently flowing within earshot of his meditation – should Christ's Second Coming occur during his lifetime ('The Dawning'); he mentions 'this late, long heat' and gives a description of a local drought in dramatic hermetical terms, chiding mankind for refusing to receive nature's message ('The Tempest'). There is a ready explanation for these unusual gestures in Vaughan's poems, which were originally written as private devotions: as the poet is conferring with himself in the presence of God, his interlocutor is presumed to be omniscient. But the explanation does not diminish the originality.

It is particularly on the basis of the immediacy of the natural environment and the experiential devotion of his poetry that Henry Vaughan's literary reputation has risen during the past two centuries; and these are the qualities that have made 'The Water-fall' one of his most popular works. He begins by engaging a waterfall in direct address:

> With what deep murmurs through time's silent stealth
> Doth thy transparent, cool and watery wealth
>   Here flowing fall,
>   And chide, and call,
> As if his liquid, loose retinue stayed
> Ling'ring, and were of this steep place afraid,
>   The common pass
>   Where, clear as glass,
>   All must descend
>   Not to an end:
> But quickened by this deep and rocky grave,
> Rise to a longer course more bright and brave.

The felt proximity of Vaughan's use of 'thy' in line two and 'here' in line three, and perhaps even more the onomatopoeic intensity of his verbal painting, make this poem, embedded as it is in a concluding sequence of lyrics on themes of death and resurrection, such a vividly symbolic and convincingly

Waterfall in Ystradfellte in the Brecon Beacons (photograph courtesy Logaston Press)

personal piece. The use of longer and shorter lines suggests falling water visually and mortal reluctance emotionally; and when the following lines resolve into steady tetrameter couplets, the form once more epitomizes the content, in this case the long cascade of verse embodies the stream of reflections on the implicit moral lessons and spiritual usefulness of falling water.

> Dear stream! dear bank, where often I
> Have sat, and pleased my pensive eye,
> Why, since each drop of thy quick store
> Runs thither, whence it flowed before,
> Should poor souls fear a shade or night,
> Who came (sure) from a sea of light?
> Or since those drops are all sent back
> So sure to thee, that none doth lack,
> Why should frail flesh doubt any more
> That what God takes, he'll not restore?
> O useful element and clear!
> My sacred wash and cleanser here,[1]
> My first consigner unto those
> Fountains of life, where the Lamb[2] goes!
> What sublime truths, and wholesome themes,
> Lodge in thy mystical, deep streams!
> Such as dull man can never find
> Unless that Spirit lead his mind,
> Which first upon thy face did move,
> And hatched all with his quickening love.[3]

[1] a reference to the sacrament of baptism. [2] that is, Christ. [3] an allusion to the Creation, when the Holy Spirit brought the world to life.

The glance toward God's original contact with Creation, presented under Vaughan's favoured hermetic description of divine incubation, leads the poet to consider the end of earthly life and the prospective return to the eternal: here the direct address to the waterfall abruptly ends, and the poet's thoughts emulate the stream, passing away to seek their spiritual origin in the supernatural 'sea of light':

> As this loud brook's incessant fall
> In streaming rings restagnates[1] all,
> Which reach by course the bank, and then
> Are no more seen, just so pass men.
> O my invisible estate,
> My glorious liberty,[2] still late!
> Thou art the channel my soul seeks,
> Not this with cataracts and creeks.

[1] regains stillness. [2] the soul's freedom from the material world.

The River Usk looking south-east (photograph by Philip Coyne)

The ending of 'The Water-fall' is a good vantage point from which to ask a question often posed since the recovery of Vaughan's texts in the mid-nineteenth century: is Henry Vaughan a nature poet? The general consensus is that he is not – at least, not in the sense that Wordsworth was. His poetic manifesto, the 1654 Preface to *Silex Scintillans*, makes not a single gesture toward the rendering of nature as a poetic goal. Yet unquestionably he is a poet who aims to 'shine like the stars for ever and ever', and who flourishes with readers still 'not with *leaf* only, but with some *fruit* also'. Having given up his early secular goal of becoming the tutelary poetic spirit of the River Usk, Vaughan achieved instead a transfiguration of his specific local landscape, making of the Usk Valley a mystical literary prototype of all nature, a visionary book accessible to readers worldwide. Modernity now seems to have granted some anticipatory affirmation to the prayer at the close of his poem 'The Book':

> O knowing, glorious spirit![1] when
> Thou shalt restore trees, beasts and men,
> When thou shalt make all new again,
> Destroying only death and pain,
> Give him amongst thy works a place,
> Who in them loved and sought thy face!

[1] that is, God the creator and redeemer.

Vanity of Spirit

Quite spent[1] with thoughts I left my cell, and lay
Where a shrill spring tuned to the early day.

   I begged here long, and groaned to know
   Who gave the clouds so brave[2] a bow,
   Who bent the spheres,[3] and circled in
   Corruption with this glorious ring,
   What is his name, and how I might
   Descry some part of his great light.
I summoned nature: pierced through all her store,
Broke up some seals, which none had touched before,
   Her womb, her bosom, and her head
   Where all her secrets lay a bed
   I rifled quite, and having passed
   Through all the creatures, came at last
   To search my self, where I did find
   Traces, and sounds of a strange kind.
Here of this mighty spring,[4] I found some drills,[5]
With echoes beaten from the eternal hills;
   Weak beams, and fires flashed to my sight,
   Like a young east,[6] or moon-shine night,
   Which showed me in a nook cast by
   A piece of much antiquity,
   With hieroglyphics quite dismembered,
   And broken letters scarce remembered.
I took them up, and (much joyed,) went about
T' unite those pieces, hoping to find out
   The mystery; but this near done,
   That little light[7] I had was gone:
   It grieved me much. At last, said I,
   Since in these veils[8] my eclipsed eye
   May not approach thee, (for at night
   Who can have commerce with the light?)
   I'll disapparel,[9] and to buy
   But one half glance, most gladly die.

[1] worn out. [2] splendid. [3] the spheres on which stars and planets were thought to be carried round the earth. [4] the power of the creator of the universe. [5] small streams. [6] early dawn. [7] the light of reason. [8] of the flesh. [9] undress, that is, discard my human body.

This poem from the 1650 *Silex Scintillans* begins with questions about some of the wonders of the created universe; in the second stanza, the poet investigates the natural world in the manner of a hermetic or scientific researcher, perhaps echoing his twin brother's anxiety that he has prostituted and diminished the 'Majesty' of Nature by 'having almost broken her Seale, and exposed her naked to the World' (*Anima Magica Abscondita*), and concludes by probing the secrets of his own inner being; and in the third stanza, he gains a few 'weak' flashes of insight and discovers an indecipherable piece 'of much antiquity', which may have been suggested by a cromlech in the neighbouring parish of Llanhamlach – a prehistoric stone structure, covered in crosses, circles, and other 'hieroglyphics' – but which has been interpreted as a symbol for the defaced image of God in his own soul. In the final stanza, he tries vainly to restore this broken image until he recognizes that the 'little light' of human reason is inadequate to the task of delving into the 'mystery' of the God who made the rainbow and the human soul. Since even a 'half glance' at the Creator can be obtained only by casting aside the material existence that blinds his earthly 'eye', he prays for the release of his spirit in death.

The Timber

Sure thou didst flourish once! and many springs,
Many bright mornings, much dew, many showers
Passed o'er thy head: many light *hearts* and *wings*
Which now are dead, lodged[1] in thy living bowers.

And still a new succession[2] sings and flies;
Fresh groves grow up, and their green branches shoot
Towards the old and still enduring skies,
While the low *violet* thrives at their root.

But thou beneath the sad and heavy *line*[3]
Of death, dost waste[4] all senseless, cold and dark;
Where not so much as dreams of light may shine,
Nor any thought of greenness, leaf or bark.

And yet (as if some deep hate and dissent,
Bred in thy growth[5] betwixt high winds and thee,
Were still alive) thou dost great storms resent[6]
Before they come, and know'st how near they be.

Else all at rest thou liest, and the fierce breath
Of tempests can no more disturb thy ease;
But this thy strange resentment[7] after death
Means[8] only those, who broke (in life) thy peace.

So murdered man, when lovely life is done,
And his blood freezed, keeps in the centre still
Some secret sense, which makes the dead blood run
At his approach, that did the body kill.

And is there any murderer worse than sin?
Or any storms more foul than a lewd life?

Or what *resentient*⁹ can work more within,
Than true remorse, when with past sins at strife?
He that hath left life's vain joys and vain care,
And truly hates to be detained on earth,
Hath got an house where many mansions¹⁰ are,
And keeps his soul unto eternal mirth.

But though thus dead unto the world, and ceased
From sin, he walks a narrow, private way;
Yet grief and old wounds make him sore displeased,
And all his life a rainy, weeping day.¹¹

For though he should forsake the world, and live
As mere a stranger, as men long since dead;
Yet joy it self will make a right soul grieve
To think, he should be so long vainly led.

But as shades set off light, so tears and grief
(Though of themselves but a sad blubbered story)
By showing the sin great, show the relief
Far greater, and so speak my Saviour's glory.

If my way lies through deserts and wild woods;
Where all the land with scorching heat is cursed;
Better, the pools should flow with rain and floods
To fill my bottle,¹² than I die with thirst.

Blest showers they are, and streams sent from above
Begetting *virgins* where they use to flow;¹³
And trees of life no other waters love,
These upper springs and none else make them grow.

But these chaste fountains flow not till we die;
Some drops may fall before, but a clear spring
And ever running, till we leave to fling
Dirt in her way,¹⁴ will keep above the sky.

St Paul's Epistle to the Romans, Chapter 6, verse 7: 'He that is dead, is freed from sin.'

---

¹ nested. ² generation of birds. ³ limit. ⁴ rot. ⁵ while the tree was still growing. ⁶ detect, feel again. ⁷ act of feeling something, with a pun on the modern meaning of resent. ⁸ refers to. ⁹ something which causes a change of feeling. ¹⁰ apartments in heaven (an allusion to the words of Jesus in John's gospel 14: 2: 'In my Father's house are many mansions'). ¹¹ the wounds of former sins make him weep. ¹² with tears of repentance. ¹³ an idea derived from the Vulgate (Latin) bible. ¹⁴ till we leave behind this earthly body (which defiles our souls).

This poem breaks into two unequal parts: the first five stanzas evoke the life and death of a fallen tree; the sixth stanza (by way of a piece of folklore about murder) marks a transition from observation of nature to moral reflection; and the last eight stanzas dwell upon the need to repent for past sins until the soul is released from the body in death. In the first book-length study of Vaughan, published in 1927, the poet Edmund Blunden lamented that the sublimity of the opening was ruined by the moralizing of the close. Later critics have praised Vaughan's ability to feel his way into the experience of the tree but regretted that the religious lessons drawn from this exercise of empathy tend to dissipate its poetic energy. More recently, commentators have emphasized Vaughan's awareness that a tract of woodland is a 'biosphere', in which trees provide habitation for generations of birds, fall and decompose, and so create the conditions for the growth of 'fresh groves' and the lowly 'violet'. The epigraph from St Paul, however, suggests that sin and repentance were at the heart of Vaughan's poetic vision from the beginning; but rather than complaining that the moral reflection spoils the richly imaginative address to the tree, it might be fairer to the poet's seventeenth-century culture and sensibility to admire the skill with which he brings into creative contact two vital elements of his experience: the 'intuitive' (which looks forward to both Romantic and ecological developments in Western culture) and the 'devotional' (which was firmly grounded in established habits of Christian meditation).

The Book

Eternal God! maker of all
That have lived here, since the man's[1] fall;
The Rock of ages! in whose shade
They live unseen, when here they fade.[2]

Thou knew'st this *paper*, when it was
Mere *seed*, and after that but grass;
Before 'twas *dressed* or *spun*, and when
Made *linen*, who did *wear* it then:
What were their lives, their thoughts & deeds
Whether good *corn*, or fruitless *weeds*.[3]

Thou knew'st this *tree*, when a green *shade*
Covered it, since a *cover* made,
And where it flourished, grew and spread,
As if it never should be dead.

Thou knew'st this harmless *beast*, when he
Did live and feed by thy decree
On each green thing; then slept (well fed)

Clothed with this *skin*, which now lies spread
A *covering* o'er this aged book,
Which makes me wisely weep and look
On my own dust; mere dust it is,
But not so dry and clean as this.
Thou knew'st and saw'st them all and though
Now scattered thus, dost know them so.[4]

O knowing, glorious spirit! When
Thou shalt restore trees, beasts and men,[5]
When thou shalt make all new again,
Destroying only death and pain,
Give him[6] amongst thy works[7] a place,
Who in them loved and sought thy face!

[1] Adam's. [2] Christ is the rock that shelters all living creatures after their death. [3] an allusion to the parable of the wheat and the tares in Matthew 13: 24-30 and John 12: 24. [4] the Creator knows grass, tree, and beast even in their present state as parts of a book. [5] Vaughan believed that everything God had made would be restored to its former condition at the end of time. [6] the poet. [7] the whole of Creation made by God.

This poem, printed towards the end of the 1655 *Silex Scintillans*, has been read as an early example of the recent ecological emphasis on the cost of our common artefacts to the environment which we exploit in order to manufacture them. In it, Vaughan meditates on the fate of everything through the ages that has been made by God the Creator, and kept safe after death by Christ the Redeemer, until the day of restoration when Christ will return and all will be made new. This combination of Christian and hermetic ideas focuses on the material ingredients that went into the construction of a book he holds in his hands: the paper, fabricated out of old clothes made from linen that was itself made by dressing and spinning flax (the 'grass' of the sixth line), which had begun life as a seed; the wooden boards of the cover, derived from a tree that had once flourished and provided shade; and the skin of the animal (calf or sheep) attached to the boards as an outer cover. Comparing the dust from which his own body is made and to which it will return, the poet thinks of the God who knows and keeps a tally of all his creatures, even though they are scattered in death like the components of this ancient volume. In the last section, he prays that he will be included in the final restoration along with all other created things – the Book of Nature in which he has tried to 'read' the face of the Creator.

6
'New Cordials, new Cathartics': Henry Vaughan the Physician

Simone Thomas

I

At Llansantffraed Church, a narrow path takes the visitor to the top of the graveyard where a gravestone reads, 'Henricus Vaughan, Siluris M.D.' How Vaughan came to be a Doctor of Medicine has puzzled many. Gwenllian Morgan and Louise Guiney, who carried out a great deal of research into his life and work in the early twentieth century, could find no evidence of any formal training; and F.E. Hutchinson, whose 1947 biography of Vaughan made use of the material they had carefully collected, had no more success and could only assume that he must have been 'a medical graduate of a British or continental university', but that 'he may have begun to practice without a degree'.[(24)]

In 1655, Vaughan advised the readers of his translation of Heinrich Nolle's *Hermetical Physick* (1613) not to be offended by 'this *Hermeticall* Theorie', and added, 'For my owne part, I honour the truth where ever I find it, whether in an old, or a new Booke, in *Galen*, or in *Paracelsus*.' This volume was followed in 1657 by a translation of Nolle's *Chymist's Key* (1615), which was introduced in an epistle 'To the Reader' by Thomas Vaughan. These two translations were presumably undertaken as part of his early medical training. Nolle was a Doctor of Philosophy and Medicine of the hermetic kind, which was devoted to scientific research with a religious philosophy underlying its theories. For example, he not only cautions the physician to '*carefully observe a just Dose in all his Medicines, with respect had to their operations, and to the strength of the Patient*', but also insists that a physician '*that desires to cure sick persons well and happily, must be a sound Christian, and truly religious and holy*'. Initially this 'piety' in the hermetic writings may have been attractive to Vaughan; and his twin brother, Thomas, combined alchemical experiments with the new 'iatrochemical' approach of applying chemistry to medical theory. Various references, however, show that Henry was broad-minded and remained sympathetic to traditional herbal medicine as well as taking an interest in the contemporary medical and scientific research of William Harvey (known for establishing the circulation of the blood), Robert Boyle (a physicist now known for Boyle's Law), and Thomas Sydenham (sometimes known as the English Hippocrates).

An early interest in the healing art is indicated by the translation of two short treatises by Plutarch and Maximus Tyrius, both of them entitled *Of the Diseases of the Mind and the Body*, in *Olor Iscanus* (1651). After a period of intense poetic activity following the deaths of his brother, William, in 1648 and King Charles I in 1649, Vaughan suffered a prolonged bout of illness from 1652 to 1654. In a dedicatory letter to his collection of prose translations, *Flores Solitudinis* (1654), he excuses any imperfections in the volume with the information that '*a peevish, inconstant state of health would not suffer me to stay for greater performances, or a better season*'; and in the 1655 edition of *Silex Scintillans*, he claims in a preface dated 30 September 1654 that he has been '*nigh unto death*' and is '*still at no great distance from it*'. It was at that time, when completing his collection of devotional poetry, that he probably started a serious study of medicine, perhaps as a result of his own poor health. In *Silex Scintillans* there are various medical metaphors, such as 'eye salve', 'salves and syrups', 'new Cordials, new Cathartics', 'a sugerd Dosis of Wormwood', 'pills', the instruction to 'spit out their phlegm', and allusions to the medical use of dead flowers.

II

Although there is no contemporary evidence of Vaughan's early career as a doctor, on 15 June 1673 he wrote a letter to his cousin John Aubrey in which he affirmed, 'My profession allso is physic, wch I have practised now for many years with good successe (I thank god!) and a repute big enough for a person of greater parts than my selfe.' From 1677, he was consistently described as a doctor; and in legal documents dated 1677 and 1691, he is given the title (in Latin) of Doctor of Medicine. There are also references to him attending the sick in the vicinity of Llansantffraed and further afield, so it must be assumed that he was self-taught, which was not unusual at that time. Apart from studying at a university for a medical degree, it was also possible to obtain one by a grant from the Archbishop of Canterbury, but there was no archbishop between 1645 and 1660. Some evidence does survive, however, of the means by which he acquired his medical knowledge and of the kind of medicine he practised. In the 1950s, several years after the publication of Hutchinson's biography, Edwin Wolf discovered some of Vaughan's surviving medical and scientific books at the Library Company of Philadelphia. Fourteen medical books in Latin had found their way there via a Dr William Logan (d.1758), a Bristol physician who picked them up at an auction after Vaughan died. Dr Logan bequeathed his library of thirteen hundred volumes to another William Logan (d.1776), whose father James was an avid collector of books and secretary to William Penn, founder of the state of Pennsylvania. Vaughan's medical books were subsequently passed on to James Logan, whose private library was the largest in colonial America and who was an early benefactor of the Library Company of Philadelphia.

Most of the books were used for reference by Vaughan and contain fly leaf notes and annotations in a hand identical to the one used in his extant letters. Nine of the volumes have been signed by Vaughan and one is dated 1654, coinciding with the likely start of his medical studies. They are mostly very rare and are written by reputable authors. They cover a variety of subjects and provide a balanced foundation covering traditional Galenic medicine based on the four humours as well as the teaching of Hippocrates, known as the founder of medicine. The collection is described and analysed in an article by Donald Dickson, published in *Scintilla* in 2005, from which the following details are taken.

The two most heavily annotated volumes were both in the tradition of humours medicine associated with Galen. One was Nicolaas Fonteyn's *De puerorum morbis* (1642), which was autographed by Vaughan in 1654 and contains his notes on four of the fly-leaves. This pocket-sized book, by a Dutchman who studied in Rheims and worked at the Medical College in Amsterdam, recommended Galenic and Hippocratic treatments of children's diseases, such as methods of evacuating 'delinquent humours' and a tonic to alleviate melancholia. Fonteyn was also the author of *The Womans Doctour* (1644, translated into English in 1652), which discussed illnesses affecting virgins, whose blood was thought to thicken, causing insomnia, melancholia and depression. The second book, the *Aphorisms* of Hippocrates edited by Johannes Tilemann in 1650, also contains Vaughan's signature, underscoring in the text, and notes and prescriptions for herbal purges and syrups in the fly-leaves. This was a handy reference book describing the skills of observation, diagnosis and treatment, together with a discussion of Galen's view that a balance of the four fluids or humours must be maintained in a healthy body. Tilemann had added to the Hippocratic material an index organized anatomically for easy reference and some of his own formulas, which included chemical medicines as well as traditional Galenic recipes. But although Vaughan was attracted by the hermetic approach, the authority of the long tradition of Hippocrates, whose writings were available in print across Europe at that time, meant that this was likely to have formed the basis of his own practice. For example, the recipe for a purgative draught for bilious liver disease includes raisins, violet flowers, borage, veronica, thyme, senna, and rhubarb to be steeped in barley water.

Reference to an up-to-date book on herbal remedies confirms the accuracy of such prescriptions.

Some of the other books contain fewer notes and signatures. For example, François Bayle's *Tractatus de apoplexia* (1678), written by a man who held the chair of medicine at Toulouse, describes apoplexy or a stroke as being due to arteriosclerosis of the cerebral blood vessels; and a marginal note in one of the other books bound with it confirms Vaughan's interest in this subject. In *De arcanis medicorum* by Hermann Grube, published in 1673, Vaughan signed the title page and compiled a table of contents on the end fly-leaf. Grube was a physician from Schleswig Holstein who opposed superstition, 'signatures' of plants (marks supposedly indicating their medicinal qualities), and the use of magic in medicine and endorsed Harvey's discovery of the circulation of the blood. Although open to new ideas, he remained in the tradition of Galen. Johann Hochstetter, a professor of medicine in Basel, published a series of one hundred cases compiled over a ten year period in *Rararum Observationum medicinalium decades sex* (1674), describing different diseases and their treatments, including observations, investigations, and advice for others. He defends iatrochemistry in a preface and pours scorn on the 'Methodical Dogmatists' who marched under the banner of Galen and Hippocrates. The 1675 edition of Wolfgang Hofer's *Hercules medicus* – inscribed 'Vaughan-76' – is a large volume organized into sections covering apoplexy, paralysis, thorax, viscera, arteries, skin, fevers, women's and children's diseases, as well as case notes covering hyperthyroidism. Vaughan made a single note in the margin about the dryness of fevers and highlighted a cure for a quartan fever. Johann Lotichius, from Frankfurt, was a poet like Vaughan and believed in natural marvels, signatures of plants, and the virtues of constellations. His *Consiliorum et observationum medicinalium libri VI* (1644) offered case studies with observations and treatments, including herbal remedies, and was usefully organized like a modern anatomy. The first chapter covered fevers, the second the head and nervous system, the third the thorax and lungs, the fourth the heart and kidneys, the fifth the female organs, and the sixth miscellaneous problems.

Quadripartitum botanicum de simplicium medicamentorum facultatibus by Simon Paulli, published in 1667-8 and signed 'Vaughan-82, pretium 12s.' on the title page, was a detailed herbal of over 700 pages on medical pharmacology, arranged into an almanac according to the seasons. In his copy, Vaughan supplied the common English names for nearly two thirds of the plants. For example, he wrote of *alysson*, 'A forreign plant, or shrub: whose very sight or touch cures those who have been bitten by mad dogs.' A note on the front fly-leaf of Jean Pecquet's *Experimenta nova anatomica* (1651) indicates that it was bought by Thomas Vaughan the year after it was published.

He must have passed it on to his brother, who made a number of annotations. Dickson describes this as the most significant book in Vaughan's extant library 'from the perspective of modern medicine', since Pecquet dissected live animals and substantiated Harvey's theory of the circulation of the blood. He also made discoveries in his work on the lymphatic system and the causes of fevers. Johann Conrad Peyer from Basel also conducted animal experiments to demonstrate the lymphatic system in the walls of the ileum; in Vaughan's copy of his *Parerga anatomica et medica, septem* (1682), there are annotations questioning some of his conclusions, showing both the poet's careful reading and his willingness to challenge other practitioners. Giovanni Sinibaldi's *Geneanthropeiae sive de hominis generatione decateuchon* (1669), acquired in 1676, is a volume of nearly a thousand pages on human sexual anatomy and physiology, to which Vaughan added his own index on the fly leaf. The cures give an insight into the private lives of Vaughan's patients in rural Wales. To curb the flow of menses, there were several treatments including the special use of dried fruits and Montagnana's pills (based in gold leaf from the early fifteenth-century Italian physician). To suppress the libido, camphor in lemon juice was used and opiates were prescribed as remedies for gonorrhea. To strengthen the uterus in labour, plaster of Mercatus was administered. Whilst some of his remedies followed Galenic theories, the majority were based on sound principles of observation and experimentation. Finally, Bernhard Verzascha's *Observationum medicarum centuria* (1677) was the work of a herbalist from Basel, who was amongst the first to study the effect of poisonous plants such as hemlock on animals. He also wrote about the toxicology of arsenic, antimony and mercury as medicines.

These are only a handful of the books that Vaughan may have used. Dickson cites evidence that 'between 1649 and 1659 over 163 self-help books aimed at the lay public were published in English'.[25] Most of these would have been herbals and would have been more common and readily available than the Latin volumes that found their way to Philadelphia. Vaughan may well have been exposed to such books and remedies from an early age at home. Nothing in the books that have survived from his personal library suggests that he adopted the new iatrochemical principles in his own practice of medicine, which was almost certainly based on the traditional herbal remedies administered by other country doctors of the age. Further information about some of the herbs mentioned by Vaughan and their uses is displayed on the information boards on the 'Vaughan Walk' and at the Vaughan garden near Talybont-on-Usk.

III

References in letters written by Vaughan confirm his good reputation as a physician with the well-to-do across a considerable geographical area. Writing to his cousin John Aubrey on 15 June 1673, he explains, 'Yours of the 10th of June I received att Breckon, where I am still attending our Bishops Lady in a tertian feaver, & cannot as yet have the leasure to step home.' In 1680, Aubrey wrote that his cousin 'has the Practice of Physic all over those Parts' and a short while later that Vaughan 'has a great and steady practice there'. In another letter, from Crickhowell dated 14 September 1693, Vaughan excuses himself from attending a summons from the Judge of the Brecon circuit on the grounds of his 'present engagement with Mr Serjeant Le Hunts Lady, who is most dangerously sick in a putrid fever with most malignant symptoms'. On 9 December 1675, he wrote from further afield, 'your letter of 27th of November I received butt last week, my occasions in Glamorganshire having detained me there the best part of the month'. These 'occasions' are likely to have been professional calls upon his medical services.

It may be appropriate to conclude this chapter on Vaughan as a reputable if self-taught physician with Louise Guiney's evocative flight of fancy, quoted in Hutchinson's chapter on 'Henry Vaughan, Doctor in Physic':

> One can picture him on his hardy Welsh pony, drenched in the mountain mists, close-hatted, big-cloaked, riding alone and looking abroad with those mild eyes which were a naturalist's for earth and sky, and a mystic's for the spiritual world.[(26)]

Affliction (I)

Peace, peace; it is not so.[1] Thou dost miscall
   Thy physic; pills that change
Thy sick accessions[2] into settled health,
This is the great *elixir*[3] that turns gall
To wine, and sweetness; poverty to wealth,
   And brings man home, when he doth range.[4]
Did not he,[5] who ordained the day,
    Ordain night too?
And in the greater world display
What in the lesser he would do?[6]
All flesh is clay, thou know'st; and but that God
   Doth use his rod,
And by a fruitful change of frosts, and showers
   Cherish, and bind thy *powers*,
Thou wouldst to weeds, and thistles quite disperse,

And be more wild than is thy verse;
Sickness is wholesome, and crosses[7] are but curbs
   To check the mule, unruly man,
They are heaven's husbandry, the famous fan
   Purging the floor which chaff disturbs.[8]
Were all the year one constant sun-shine, we
      Should have no flowers,
All would be drought, and leanness; not a tree
      Would make us bowers;
Beauty consists in colours; and that's best
   Which is not fixed, but flies, and flows;
The settled *red* is dull, and *whites* that rest
   Something of sickness would disclose.
   Vicissitude plays all the game,
      Nothing that stirs,
      Or hath a name,
   But waits upon this wheel,[9]
Kingdoms too have their physic, and for steel,[10]
   Exchange their peace, and furs,
Thus doth God *key*[11] disordered man,
   (Which none else can,)
   Tuning his breast to rise, or fall;
   And by a sacred, needful art
   Like strings, stretch every part
   Making the whole most musical.

[1] the poet silences an inner voice. [2] attacks of illness. [3] in alchemy, that which turns base metals into gold; in medicine, a drug to cure disease. [4] go astray. [5] God. [6] the greater world is the macrocosm; the lesser is the microcosm, man. [7] afflictions. [8] an allusion to the biblical image of winnowing the grain from the chaff (the righteous from the sinful). [9] of fortune. [10] weaponry; war purges states grown lethargic in peace. [11] tune.

This is one of the few poems by Vaughan in which sickness and its cure provide both theme and metaphor. George Herbert has five poems with the title 'Affliction' and Vaughan may be glancing at these and offering a more positive interpretation of the role of sickness in human life. Like alternations of night and day or bad weather and good, sickness and health are part of the divine dispensation that regulates the universe. Towards the end, he applies the same analysis to the world of politics, perhaps glancing at the Civil War in contemporary Britain.

Begging (II)

Aye, do not go![1] thou know'st, I'll die!
My *Spring* and *Fall* are in thy book![2]
Or, if thou goest, do not deny
To lend me, though from far, one look!

My sins long since have made thee strange,
A very stranger unto me;
No morning-meetings since this change,
Nor evening-walks have I with thee.

Why is my God thus slow and cold,
When I am most, most sick and sad?[3]
Well fare those blessed days of old
When thou didst hear the *weeping lad*![4]

O do not thou do as I did,
Do not despise a love-sick heart!
What though some cloud's defiance bid[5]
Thy Sun must shine in every part.

Though I have spoiled, O spoil not thou!
Hate not thine own dear gift and token![6]
Poor birds sing best, and prettiest show,
When their nest is fall'n and broken.

Dear Lord! restore thy ancient peace,
Thy quickening friendship, man's bright wealth!
And if thou wilt not give me ease
From sickness, give my spirit health!

[1] addressed to God. [2] the Book of Life in Revelation, Chapter 20, verse 12. [3] his spiritual condition as well as his physical sickness. [4] Ishmael in Genesis, saved by God from dying of thirst in the desert. [5] even if a cloud (such as ill health) tries to hide the light of God. [6] the gift of life to human beings.

This poem was probably written when Vaughan was suffering from a serious and prolonged illness during the 1650s At that time, he was writing many of the poems published in 1655 in the second part of *Silex Scintillans*, hence his reference to birds 'singing best' in affliction.

7
'Such low & forgotten thinges': The Vaughan Heritage

Elizabeth Siberry

I

Henry Vaughan would not recognize Llansantffraed Church today, although, A40 apart, he would see a familiar landscape setting. Some rebuilding took place in 1690, and in 1884-5 the old church, which was in a poor state of repair, was taken down and rebuilt by the Rhayader-based architect Stephen Williams. A series of watercolours, however, provide a record of what the old church might have looked like.

Llansantffraed Church, watercolour *c.*1884 (courtesy Brecknock Museum)

In the late eighteenth century, the Revd John Swete, a historian and antiquary of the county of Devon, travelled through Wales and painted Llansantffraed Church with its distinctive pepperpot tower. Four other watercolours, by an unknown hand, dating probably from just before the complete rebuild, are in the collections of the National Library of Wales, the Brecknock Museum and the church itself. A few fragments of the old church, such as the font and carved window head stone, were also retained and can still be seen today.

The memory of Vaughan himself also faded with time. When he answered John Aubrey's request for information about the lives and literary works of himself and his deceased twin brother in 1673, he was aware that he and Thomas were passing out of the public consciousness: 'I am highly obliged to you that you would be pleased to remember, & reflect vpon such low & forgotten thinges, as my brother and my selfe.' And although he figured briefly in the 1721 English edition of the *Athenae Oxonienses* (an account of Oxford graduates) compiled by Anthony Wood, on whose behalf Aubrey had made his original inquiries, he was almost entirely unknown to the eighteenth century. Theophilus Jones, writing a history of Brecknockshire in 1805, remembered him vaguely as 'a doctor of physic' and brother of 'an experimental philosopher'. Noting that the inscription on his gravestone was 'now defaced', he gives a confused account of two poems from *Olor Iscanus*, which he seems to attribute to Thomas rather than Henry Vaughan[27]. Some time later, a poem, 'On the River Usk' by John Lloyd of Dinas, Brecon (1797-1875), quoted by Roland Mathias[28], gives the impression that Vaughan – who had celebrated the river in both Latin and English verses – was not known locally as a literary figure:

Llansantffraed Church from Talybont (photograph by Philip Coyne)

> Usk, tho' unknown to song thou may not vie
> With the famed windings of the sylvan Wye,
> With Towy glorying in her Gringar's shade,
> Or Avon sacred by a Shakespeare made;
> Yet art thou dearer far, for on thy side
> From boyhood have I stray'd, and seen thee glide
> Like a companion when none else was near
> Whisp'ring thine own sweet language on mine ear ...

There was a gradual revival of interest in Vaughan's devotional poetry during the early decades of the nineteenth century, with several of his poems being included in collections of religious verse. This culminated in the Revd H.F. Lyte's edition of *Silex Scintillans: The Sacred Poems and Private Ejaculations of Henry Vaughan* in 1847 and the Revd Alexander Grosart's complete works for the Fuller Worthies' Library in 1871. One early reader was the Prime Minister William Ewart Gladstone; his diaries note that he read Grosart's edition shortly after its publication (in November 1872 and June 1874).

Writing from Lancashire, Grosart followed Lyte in criticizing the 'culpable ignorance and blunderings of Jones in his scanty notices of our Vaughan and his brother'; and, although he acknowledged help received from Joseph Joseph of Brecon (fl.1855-90), a Fellow of the Society of Antiquaries and collector of manuscripts and documents on the history of the local area, he complained:

> The modern Welsh are astoundingly unliterary, to put it mildly. I have had simply to put aside as worthless, Welsh notices of our worthy. It were endless to correct their mistakes.[29]

Grosart added that there were more subscribers for his edition from Scotland, America, and Germany than from all Wales, which was 'ludicrous if it were not serious and sorrowful'. Grosart's work is interesting for another reason: a special illustrated edition, limited to fifty copies with illustrations by a local photographer, James Robert Griffiths of Brecon, appears to show the grave slab in an upright position.

In his *Songs of Two Worlds*, published in 1874, the Carmarthenshire poet Lewis Morris (1833-1907), a fellow alumnus of Jesus College, Oxford, addressed a poem to Vaughan as 'An Unknown Poet'; and in an article in the wonderfully named *Old Welsh Chips* in 1888, Gwenllian Morgan, a local historian and Vaughan enthusiast, lamented:

> The coldness and indifference shewn towards his works, the ignorance displayed in this, his native county, has often come to us with a sense of surprise and disappointment, his very existence being forgotten or unknown! The most striking instance of this occurred some little time ago at the reopening of the beautiful church of Llansaintfraed,

when there was a large representative gathering of the clergy and laity of the neighbourhood, and in the course of several speeches made on that occasion no single speaker mentioned the name of, or in any way referred to, Henry Vaughan.

II

A campaign to revive Vaughan's memory, however, soon began to attract attention. In the summer of 1895, the American independent scholar Louise Guiney made a special journey to visit Vaughan's grave at Llansantffraed. She was appalled by the state of his final resting place. Back home in Boston, she wrote to the London journal *The Athenaeum* on 2 October 1895:

> The slab of the tomb is broken; the Latin inscription is getting dim; under an old yew tree, probably planted there to keep the poet's dust company, and heaped all about the stone, are dead boughs, nettles, bricks, rotten wreaths, fragments of crockery, dirt and confusion unspeakable; and the parish coal-shed is so placed against the neighbouring wall that the operating genius with the shovel must stand on Henry Vaughan's burial place, and shower it with eternal slag and soot. ... Now – and this is why I wrote – cannot something be done?... Will you not find out by a public appeal, whether a few pounds cannot be put together and devoted to having the coal-shed moved, clearing the rubbish from the grave, planting a small grass plot, and keeping the spot for ever in decent and fitting condition. ...The Rector ... would be

Drawing of Henry Vaughan's grave from *The Daily Graphic*, 1895
(courtesy National Museum of Wales)

glad to have a small memorial brass to place on the chancel wall, which would be very nice and proper.

Guiney's travelling companion and later biographer, Alice Brown, wrote of the trip and subsequent campaign:

> She trod the paths her poet loved, and she was also with him, where her mind would ever be, in the seventeenth century. This was one of her ardent quests, her passionate rescues: for Vaughan was forgotten on his own familiar ground. Literally the places that had known him knew him no more. Even his grave has been desecrated by the slow attrition of neglect. A coal shed had encroached on it, coal had fallen on his stone, cans and broken glass littered the sacred spot. The two Americans ... cleared the stone with hands and walking sticks, and Louise Guiney drew to her two bent and blear-eyed Hodges working near and preached to them Vaughan, the good physician and his right to the seemliness of an ordered resting-place.[30]

An engraving of the overgrown grave, now horizontal, was published in the *Daily Graphic* on 8 November 1895.

Guiney's plea was picked up by Gwenllian Morgan, who became the Honorary Secretary of a fund that provided for the repair of the tomb and the tidying up of the ground around it, with a report published in the *Western Mail* on 11 May 1897. The statement of account of the fund accounts is preserved amongst the Gwenllian Morgan papers in the National Library of Wales and

Photograph showing Vaughan's gravestone upright
(from the Revd Grosart edition of the Complete Poems, 1871)

shows that £42 17s 6d was raised from over forty contributors throughout Britain and North America. The work was completed by Easter 1897 when, on the 202nd anniversary of the poet's death, a memorial tablet, surrounded by a deeply carved wreath of oak leaves and acorns in pink Penarth alabaster, was placed on the south wall of the nave. Both the work on the grave and the tablet were executed by Mr W. Clarke of Llandaff; a firm which remains in business today. The inscription was composed by Dean Vaughan of Llandaff, one of the main subscribers to the fund:

> In late but reverent remembrance of a sweet psalmist of Israel Henry Vaughan M.D. (known as the Silurist) of Newton by Usk in this parish who died April 23rd AD 1695 aged 73 years and was buried in this churchyard.
> "He that hath left life's vain joys and vain care.
> Hath got an house where many mansions are."

1896
Silex Scintillans

In 1925 the University of Wales granted Morgan the honorary degree of M.A. in recognition both of her civic work (she was the first female Mayor of Brecon and involved in many local causes and projects) and of her researches into the life of Vaughan. Over the years, she and Guiney corresponded regularly and planned a joint edition of Vaughan's works. Their extensive researches were, however, pre-empted by others, with a 'Muses' Library' edition of Vaughan's poems by E.K. Chambers appearing in 1896 and L.C. Martin's standard edition of *The Works of Henry Vaughan*, published by Oxford University Press, in 1914 (subsequently revised in the second edition of 1957). Louise Guiney

Louise Guiney

Gwenllian Morgan

did publish a single-volume edition of the prose work *The Mount of Olives* (1902) and a number of articles on Vaughan's life and work.

Guiney made her last visit to Vaughan's grave in April 1920 and described the scene in a letter to Gwenllian Morgan dated 20 April:

> The countryside was beautiful and peaceful, exactly as I saw it a quarter of a century ago almost to the day. Nor did I feel any change in myself or in my love for H. V. ... The tomb is sinking slightly on one side. It looks as though pilgrims had begun to go there, for inside the iron rings is quite a trodden path ... Some day I must see it all again.

In that September, however, she was taken ill whilst staying at Clytha Cottage, Abergavenny, and she died in Chipping Campden on 2 November 1920. Her grave can still be seen in Wolvercote cemetery, Oxford.

F.E. Hutchinson used the two friends' research extensively in his 1947 biography of Vaughan. In his preface, he notes that, after Gwenllian Morgan's death in 1939, her friends asked him to review her extensive collection of notes about Vaughan and her correspondence with Guiney. Hutchinson concluded that the notes were not easily translatable into a book but that he would write about Vaughan himself, scrupulously preserving all that was of value in the collection. He added, 'I trust that the book as it now stands will honour the memory of two women who discovered more about the poet they loved than any previous scholars have done.'[31] Morgan's papers at the National Library of Wales also include a number of poems, which presumably she had either collected or which had been sent to her by fellow enthusiasts, inspired by visits to Vaughan's grave, including another subscriber to the fund, Isobel Southall of Edgbaston:

The Grave, Llansantffraed

A quiet churchyard, sloping to the west,
A mountain-girded plain where swiftly moves
Impatient Usk, thro fields and shadowy groves
To find the lowlands and his ocean rest.
Incomparable scene in splendor dressed
Of autumn, or the glittering garb of spring,
Making the heart leap with its promising
Of Eden's long-lost glories re-possessed.
And here, in peace, the Iscan poet, laid
Hard by his River and his native grove,
Oer-shadowed by a thousand summered Yew,
Awaits that Day Supreme when the 'Mild Dove'
Shed forth in vital power on all things made,
Shall fashion trees and beasts and more anew.

III

The iconic location of the grave, overlooking the Usk Valley, albeit with several centuries of tree growth, and with the lintel stone from Vaughan's house at its foot, has continued to inspire poets and other visitors.

T.S. Eliot's 1921 review of an anthology of metaphysical poetry, later included in his *Selected Essays*, was influential in reawakening critical interest in Vaughan and his forerunners and contemporaries. In 1924, the poet Siegfried Sassoon visited Vaughan's grave and, a week or so later, staying at Manorbier in Pembrokeshire, he was inspired to write a poem entitled simply 'At the grave of Henry Vaughan':

> Above the voiceful windings of a river
> An old green slab of simply graven stone
> Shuns notice, overshadowed by a yew.
> Here Vaughan lies dead, whose name flows on for ever
> Through pastures of the spirit washed with dew
> And starlit with eternities unknown
>
> Here sleeps the Silurist; the loved physician;
> The face that left no portraiture behind;
> The skull that housed white angels, and had vision
> Of daybreak through the gateways of the mind.
> Here lie faith, mercy, wisdom and humility,
> Whose influence shall prevail for evermore;
> Here, from this lowly grave, shines Heaven's tranquillity;
> And here stand I, a suppliant at the door.
>
> 27 August 1924

The poem was published in the *London Mercury* in February 1925 and then, slightly revised, in Sassoon's collection of poetry, *The Heart's Journey*, in 1927.

In 1924, the composer Gustav Holst composed a motet inspired by Vaughan's 'Dialogue between the Body and Soul', for mezzo soprano, tenor and eight part choir which Sassoon heard in Gloucester in September 1925. Vaughan's poetry has also inspired a number of other British composers, namely Sir Arthur Bliss (*The Beatitudes*); Gerald Finzi ('Welcome sweet and sacred feast'); Hubert Parry (*Songs of Farewell*); Edward Elgar's part songs, *The Fountain* and *The Shower*, and more recently John Tavener (*They are all gone into the world of light*, 2011), as well as hymns for public worship, which are in use to this day. Local choirs still perform some of these works, reflecting both revived local interest in Vaughan's life and work and the strong musical tradition of the Usk Valley.

Sassoon recalled his visit forty years later, in July 1964, when he read an article about Llansantffraed in the magazine *Country Life*. The author commented

Roland Mathias

that the grave was 'profoundly moving in its simplicity' and that 'Vaughan's beloved Usk Valley is without doubt the place where his poems may be read with greater poignancy than anywhere else, for his vision is inseparable from its setting.' This remains the case today.

The historical novel, *Swan of Usk*, by Helen Ashton, which was published in 1940, is a rather different tribute to Vaughan. Ashton (1891-1958) trained as a doctor but after her marriage gave up medicine and over some forty-three years published twenty-six books from biographies to historical novels. She highlighted the researches of Morgan and Guiney and acknowledged help from the former. Noting that circumstances prevented the completion of their long planned biography, Ashton wrote, 'I have thought myself justified in attempting what I have long wanted to write, a fictional reconstruction of Henry Vaughan's life and times.'[32] Whilst she cites a range of sources consulted, her chosen medium enables her to fill in gaps, for which there is no evidence. The style is perhaps now also rather dated but her book is certainly a Vaughan curiosity.

Another writer inspired by Vaughan's grave was Roland Mathias (1915-2007), a leading Welsh writer of the twentieth century, whose poem 'On the grave of Henry Vaughan at Llansantffraed' was published in his collection, *The Flooded Valley*, in 1960:

> Sun at arm's length, infant cajoling ball,
> And stretching finger full of hale man's blood
> This is the promise, here the hump and wall
> By which the grave yew ghosts continue longer
> And in their church of damp have hosts.
>
> In this blind parcel is the portion lost,
> The hampered reason, the most potent sin:
> Yet the prostrate endurance of this dust
> Beyond the rain's dearth, into the light season,
> Marks the exacting purpose of the earth.
>
> Man that is God and ghost, fuel and fire,
> Factor and master, ephemeral, crossed
> Peccator maximus stirring to desire,
> Dust shall have shape and sing, in the sun faster –
> This hump is Pisgah and each shoulder wing!

Anne Cluysenaar

More recently, the late Anne Cluysenaar (1936-2014), one of the founding editors of *Scintilla*, the annual publication of the Usk Valley Vaughan Association (now the Vaughan Association), wrote a sequence of poems entitled 'Vaughan Variations' (see Chapter One), which was included in her 1997 volume, *Timeslips*. In 2004, she published a selection of Vaughan's poems; and her own reflections on Vaughan's grave appeared in *Touching Distances*, published by Cinnamon Press in 2014:

> You must have seen springs like this one? A mist
> Of leafless copse, which like the river shines through.
> Hedges with blackthorn. A shadow leaning
> Across the valley from Pen-y-fan.
>
> This side, as you said, catches the last
> Light. Standing here again, embarrassed,
> unworthy as always, I think of your bones
> left here, as well as your soul.
>
> Astonishing silence. No cars. No jets.
> None of the big noises. Then slowly
> I became aware of hymning circulations
> Far and near, and the whirr of wings
>
> Folding to some nest just within earshot.
> Nothing else, for what seems no time, matters.
> But between H and E on your boundary-stone
> Someone has laid these two cuckoo-flowers.

Professor Jeremy Hooker, who has written about Vaughan and landscape in Chapter One of this volume, has also published a poem about the grave in *Scintilla* No. 17.

In 2010, the Nobel Prize-winning Irish poet, Seamus Heaney, also came to pay his respects to Henry Vaughan, in company with fellow writers Karl Miller, founder and editor of the *London Review of Books*, and the novelist Andrew O'Hagan. Their visit to Llansantffraed formed part of a literary journey which is recorded in a series of essays published by Miller in 2011 under the title *Tretower to Clyro*. In his foreword, O'Hagan writes of their visit to the grave – 'there are words in the air' – and recalls that 'Karl and Seamus sat on a bench and argued about the Latin on Vaughan's grave' and that Seamus 'spoke about Eliot and the *Four Quartets*'. Karl Miller also notes

Henry Vaughan's grave at Llansantffraed (photograph by Hywel Bevan)

that they recited Vaughan's poem, 'The Night'. And many other writers will no doubt have visited Llansantffraed without recording the details of their literary pilgrimage.

IV

This is not the place to list all the editions of Vaughan's poetry or to discuss his wider influence on other poets but it is worth mentioning that his work has attracted the interest of fine press printers in Wales, combining the text with artistic interpretations of his words and the local landscape. In 1924, the Gregynog Press, founded by the great patrons of art, Gwendoline and Margaret Davies at their home in rural Montgomeryshire, produced an edition of his poems, dedicated to the memory of Louise Guiney. The text was edited by Ernest Rhys, editor of Everyman's Library, with accompanying wood engravings by Robert Maynard and Horace Bray. They include charming depictions of the old church and views of the Usk Valley and the introduction notes that the 'two craftsmen or as Vaughan would say artificers most concerned in this Gregynog book set out to explore the Usk Valley and country around Brecon and Llansantffraed' in the summer of 1923. In 2009, the modern Gwasg Gregynog also produced a selection of writings of Henry and Thomas Vaughan entitled *The Texture of the Universe*, illustrated by wood engraver Hilary Paynter. And in the same year, local artist, writer and printer Shirley Jones, of Red Hen Press, published *Terra Contigua*, a 'visual response' to the poetry of Vaughan and Thomas Traherne. Vaughan's poetry has also inspired the Welsh artist Clive Hicks-Jenkins, who for many years worked at nearby Tretower Court and knows Llansantffraed Church well. In 2014, he produced a design for a stained glass window, drawing on

Clive Hicks-Jenkins' swan design

Vaughan's poetry and imagery. And another local artist, Robert Macdonald, has created an imaginary portrait of Vaughan, set against the mountains (see title page).

Since 1929, the Brecknock Society has celebrated Vaughan's life and works by holding a service in Llansantffraed Church on the Sunday nearest to the anniversary of his death on 23 April. This is now organized in conjunction with the Vaughan Association, which holds its annual colloquium over the same weekend, and the service includes both readings of Vaughan's poetry and the laying of a wreath upon his grave. The latter has recently been restored with an appeal for funds, as in 1895, drawing support from local organizations and residents as well as international Vaughan scholars. The new path and information board encourage visitors and a well-placed bench provides a tranquil spot to sit, rest, and perhaps read some of Vaughan's poetry. Refurbishment of the church in 2014, helped by the Heritage Lottery Fund, has also ensured that

The annual Vaughan service at Llansantffraed (2015)

Peter Thomas

it can remain open and play its part in celebrating Vaughan's poetry and life.

Vaughan's love of his local landscape is also commemorated in the Vaughan Walk, which was planned and developed in 2006 on the initiative of Seamus Hamill-Keays, a local resident whose house, The Allt, is just south of Llansantffraed Church. The walk, a gentle four kilometres, starts and finishes in the nearby village of Talybont-on-Usk and is marked by illustrated boards with excerpts from the poetry of both Henry and Thomas Vaughan. These were carefully selected with advice from Anne Cluysenaar and Peter Thomas from the Vaughan Association. The words, and a small herb garden on the walk, highlight both brothers' interest in plants and their use in healing (see Chapter Six by Simone Thomas, Peter Thomas's daughter and a practising GP). The walk also celebrates their love of the local landscape and especially of the water flowing through it in streams and the River Usk. And appropriately, the new building for the health practice in Brecon is named Ty Henry Vaughan.

All these local initiatives – including the present volume – are fitting and ongoing tributes to Henry Vaughan, and to the Usk Valley, which was both his home and the inspiration of his poetry.

Information boards for the Vaughan Walk

List of contributors

Jeremy Hooker is Emeritus Professor of English at the University of South Wales, and a Fellow of the Welsh Academy, and a Fellow of the Learned Society of Wales. His third journal, *Openings: A European Journal,* was published by Shearsman in 2014. His most recent collection of poems is *Scattered Light* (Enitharmon, 2015). He has published extensively on British and American poetry and the literature of place and Welsh writing in English, and his books include *Writers in a Landscape* (University of Wales Press, 1996) and *Imagining Wales: A View of Modern Welsh Writing in English* (University of Wales Press, 2001).

Jonathan Nauman, a metrologist and independent scholar from New England, often visits the United Kingdom to speak on seventeenth-century poetry. He is author of *The Franklin Trees*, a children's book, and has published articles on Henry Vaughan in *The Seventeenth Century*, *The Huntington Library Quarterly* and *Scintilla*.

Elizabeth Siberry is a local historian and regular contributor to *Brycheiniog*. She is a member of the Council of the Brecknock Society and Museum Friends and a Trustee of the Brecknock Arts Trust. She is also a Trustee of the National Library of Wales and member of the Council of the University of Wales.

Simone Thomas is the daughter of the late Peter Thomas, who was a founding member of the Usk Valley Vaughan Association and editor of *Scintilla*, the Association's journal. She practises as a GP in Somerset.

Robert Wilcher was formerly Reader in Early Modern Studies at the University of Birmingham and is an Honorary Fellow of the Shakespeare Institute in Stratford-upon-Avon. He has published books on the seventeenth-century poets Andrew Marvell and Sir John Suckling and his study of the years of civil war and interregnum, *The Writing of Royalism 1628-1660* (Cambridge University Press, 2001), provides a political and literary context for the work of Henry Vaughan. His other publications include articles and chapters on Shakespeare, seventeenth-century poetry, and Charles I's *Eikon Basilike*. He is currently one of three scholars preparing an edition of the complete works of Henry Vaughan for Oxford University Press.

Helen Wilcox is Professor of English at Bangor University and a Fellow of both the Royal Society of Literature and the English Association and is a co-editor of the journal *English*. She edited the *English Poems of George Herbert* for Cambridge University Press in 2007 and has published many essays in periodicals and collections of essays on seventeenth-century devotional writing, women's writing, and Shakespeare's tragicomedies. Among the many books she has written and edited are *Her Own Life: Autobiographical Writings by Seventeenth-Century Englishwomen* (Routledge, 1989), *George Herbert: Sacred and Profane* (Free University Press, Amsterdam, 1995), *Women and Literature in Britain, 1500-1700* (Cambridge University Press, 1996), and most recently *1611: Authority, Gender and the Word in Early Modern England* (Blackwell, 2013).

Notes on the text

These notes provide page references for quotations from secondary works. Fuller details of publication can be found in the list of Further Reading.

(1) Hutchinson, *Life and Interpretation*, p. 29.
(2) Cluysenaar, *Timeslips*, p. 131.
(3) Massingham, *The Southern Marches*, p. 99.
(4) Peter Thomas, 'The "Desert Sanctified"', pp. 168-9.
(5) Summers, *Heir of Donne and Jonson*, p. 128.
(6) Davies, *Henry Vaughan*, p. 22.
(7) Brown, *Essays and Studies* (1977), p. 57.
(8) Mathias, *Brycheiniog* 19 (1980-81), p. 29.
(9) Hutchinson, *Life and Interpretation*, p. 67.
(10) Aubrey's *Brief Lives*, p. 463.
(11) Symonds, *Diary of the Marches of the Royal Army*, p. 263.
(12) Mathias, *Scintilla* No. 2 (1998), p. 75.
(13) Dodd, *Studies in Stuart Wales*, p. 148.
(14) Wynn Thomas, *Scintilla* No. 2 (1998), p. 11.
(15) Peter Thomas, 'The "Desert Sanctified"', pp. 166-7.
(16) Quoted from the Penguin edition of Vaughan's *Complete Poems*, p. 64.
(17) West, *Scripture Uses*, p. 48.
(18) Martz, *The Paradise Within*, p. 13.
(19) Hooker, *Scintilla* No. 2 (1998), p. 141.
(20) Wynn Thomas, *Scintilla* No. 2 (1998), p. 8.
(21) Wilcher, *Scintilla* No. 15 (2011), p. 122.
(22) Guiney, 'An Oxford Poem by Henry Vaughan', p. 510.
(23) Summers, *Heirs of Donne and Jonson*, p. 121.
(24) Hutchinson, *Life and Interpretation*, p. 193.
(25) Dickson, *Scintilla* No. 9 (2005), p. 208.
(26) Quoted in Hutchinson, *Life and Interpretation*, p. 194.
(27) Jones, *History of Brecknockshire*, iii, pp. 205, 208.
(28) Mathias, *Anglo Welsh Literature*, p.43.
(29) Grosart, *Works of Henry Vaughan Silurist*, i, pp.xvi, xxii; ii, pp.342-3.
(30) Brown, *Essays and Studies* (1977), pp. 79-80.
(31) Hutchinson, *Life and Interpretation*, p. v.
(32) Ashton, *The Swan of Usk*, p. vii.

Further reading

Much has been written about Henry Vaughan since his poetry was rediscovered in the early nineteenth century and the Revd H.F. Lyte produced the first modern edition of his poetry in 1847. Pointers to further reading have been compiled from suggestions by the authors of the various chapters in this book.

A selection of Vaughan's poetry by Anne Cluysenaar was published by SPCK in 'The Golden Age of Spiritual Writing' series in 2004 and is still available.

Poetry Wales devoted a special issue to Vaughan in 1975 (Volume 11, No. 2). The first part of *The Swansea Review* No. 15 was devoted to Vaughan on the tercentenary of his death in 1995.

Brycheiniog is the journal of the Brecknock Society and Museum Friends. It is published annually and contains a number of articles relating to the Vaughan family and the history of the seventeenth century. See www.brecknocksociety.co.uk. Past copies of *Brycheiniog* up to 2003 are available through Welsh Journals Online and the website of the National Library of Wales.

The Vaughan Association (founded as The Usk Valley Vaughan Association in 1996) holds an annual colloquium at the end of April, which attracts scholars and critics from around the world. Its annual publication, *Scintilla*, contains articles about Henry and Thomas Vaughan, new poetry inspired by their vision, and discussions of other poets in a similar tradition. See www.vaughanassociation.org.

Editions

The Works of Henry Vaughan, edited by L.C. Martin [1914], 2nd edition (Clarendon Press, Oxford 1957)

Henry Vaughan: The Complete Poems, edited by Alan Rudrum (Penguin Books, 1976, revised 1983)

The Works of Thomas Vaughan, edited by Alan Rudrum (Oxford: Clarendon Press, 1984)

General

Edmund Blunden, *On the Poems of Henry Vaughan: Characteristics and Intimations* (Richard Cobden-Sanderson, London 1927)

Louis L. Martz, *The Poetry of Meditation* (Yale University Press, New Haven and London 1954, revised 1962)

E.C. Pettet, *Of Paradise and Light: A Study of Vaughan's Silex Scintillans* (Cambridge University Press, 1960)

Jonathan F.S. Post, *Henry Vaughan: The Unfolding Vision* (Princeton University Press, 1982)

Alan Rudrum, *Henry Vaughan*, 'Writers of Wales' (University of Wales Press on behalf of the Welsh Arts Council, 1981)

James D. Simmonds, *Masques of God: Form and Theme in the Poetry of Henry Vaughan* (University of Pittsburgh Press, 1972)

Joseph H. Summers, *The Heirs of Donne and Jonson* (Chatto and Windus, London 1970)

Noel Kennedy Thomas, *Henry Vaughan: Poet of Revelation* (Churchman Publishing, Worthing 1986)

Philip West, *Henry Vaughan's Silex Scintillans: Scripture Uses* (Oxford University Press, 2001)
Of Paradise and Light: Essays on Henry Vaughan and John Milton in Honor of Alan Rudrum, edited by Donald R. Dickson and Holly Faith Nelson (Newark: University of Delaware Press, 2004). Essays in this book are cited under individual chapters.

A Biographical Introduction
Brigid Allen, 'The Vaughans at Jesus College, Oxford, 1638-48', *Scintilla* No. 4 (2000), 68-78
Aubrey's Brief Lives, edited by Oliver Lawson Dick (Penguin Books, 1962), pp.463-5
Stevie Davies, *Henry Vaughan* (Seren, Poetry of Wales Press, Bridgend 1995)
Donald R. Dickson, 'The Identity of Rebecca Archer Vaughan', *Scintilla* No. 7 (2003), 129-42
F.E. Hutchinson, *Henry Vaughan: A Life and Interpretation* (Clarendon Press, Oxford 1947)
Roland Mathias, 'The Midlands: Introductions and Identifications', *Scintilla* No. 5 (2001), 93-103
C.A. Ralegh Radford, 'Tretower: The Castle and the Court', *Brycheiniog* 6 (1960), 1-50
Alan Rudrum, entry on Henry Vaughan in the *Oxford Dictionary of National Biography* (Oxford University Press, 2004).
Alan Rudrum, 'Henry Vaughan's Poems of Mourning', in *Of Paradise and Light* (2004), pp.309-28
Thomas and Rebecca Vaughan's *Aqua Vitae: Non Vitis* (British Library MS, Sloane 1741), edited and translated by Donald R. Dickson (Tempe, Arizona: Arizona Center for Medieval and Renaissance Studies, 2001)
Anthony Wood, *Historia et Antiquitates Universitatis Oxoniensis* (1674); *Athenae Oxonienses* (2nd edition, 1721)

Chapter One: Henry Vaughan in his Landscape
Eluned Brown, 'Henry Vaughan's Biblical Landscape', Essays and Studies, new series 30 (1977), 50-60
Anne Cluysenaar, 'Vaughan Variations', in *Timeslips: New and Selected Poems* (Carcanet Press, Manchester 1997)
H.J. Massingham, *The Southern Marches* (London: Robert Hale, 1952)
Roland Mathias, 'Poets of Breconshire', *Brycheiniog* 19 (1980-81), 27-49
M. Wynn Thomas, '"In Occidentem & tenebras": Putting Henry Vaughan on the Map of Wales', *Scintilla* No. 2 (1998), 7-24

Chapter Two: Henry Vaughan and the Civil Wars
E.L. Marilla, 'Henry Vaughan and the Civil War', *Journal of English and Germanic Philology* 41 (1942), 514-26
Roland Mathias, 'The Silurist Re-Examined', *Scintilla* No. 2 (1998), 62-77
Jonathan Nauman, '"To my Worthy Friend, Master T. Lewes": Vaughan, Herbert, and the Civil Wars', *Scintilla* No. 2 (1998), 128-31
Edward Parry, 'Charles I in South Wales, July to September 1645', *Brycheiniog* 29 (1996-97), 39-45
Sir Frederick Rees, 'Breconshire during the Civil War', *Brycheiniog* 8 (1962), 1-9
Richard Symonds's Diary of the Marches of the Royal Army [1859], edited by C.E. Long (Cambridge University Press, 1997)
Hugh Thomas, *A History of Wales 1485-1660* (University of Wales Press, Cardiff 1972) See Chapter 12, 'Wales and the Civil War', pp.197-216.

Robert Wilcher, *The Writing of Royalism 1628-1660* (Cambridge University Press, 2001). This book is also relevant to Chapter 3.

Chapter Three: Henry Vaughan and the Interregnum

A.H. Dodd, *Studies in Stuart Wales*, 2nd edition (University of Wales Press, Cardiff 1971). See Chapter 4, '"Nerth Y Committee"', pp.110-76.

A.M. Johnson, 'Wales during the Commonwealth and Protectorate', in *Puritans and Revolutionaries: Essays in Seventeenth-Century History Presented to Christopher Hill*, edited by Donald Pennington and Keith Thomas (Clarendon Press, Oxford 1978)

Naomi Marklew, 'Silex Scintillans: Henry Vaughan's Interregnum Elegy', *Scintilla* No. 17 (2013), 36-51

Alan Rudrum, 'Resistance, Collaboration, and Silence: Henry Vaughan and Breconshire Royalism', in *The English Civil Wars in the Literary Imagination*, edited by Claude J. Summers and Ted-Larry Pebworth (University of Missouri Press, Columbia 1999), pp.102-18

Hugh Thomas, *A History of Wales 1485-1660* (University of Wales Press, Cardiff 1972) See Chapter 13, 'Wales and the Commonwealth', pp.217-38.

Peter W. Thomas, 'The Language of Light: Henry Vaughan and the Puritans', *Scintilla* No. 3 (1999), 9-29

Chapter Four: Henry Vaughan and the Church

A.M. Allchin, '"As if Existence itself were Heavenliness": The Proximity of Paradise in Henry Vaughan and Thomas Merton', *Scintilla* No. 2 (1999), 36-53

Jeremy Hooker, 'Quickness', *Scintilla* No. 2 (1998), 141-52

Louis L. Martz, *The Paradise Within: Studies in Vaughan, Traherne, and Milton* (Yale University Press, New Haven and London 1964)

Graham Parry, 'Vaughan and Laudianism', *Scintilla* No. 13 (2009), 185-96

Claude J. Summers, 'Herrick, Vaughan, and the Poetry of Anglican Survivalism', in *New Perspectives on the Seventeenth-Century English Religious Lyric*, edited by John R. Roberts (University of Missouri Press, Columbia 1994), pp.46-73

Claude J. Summers and Ted-Larry Pebworth, 'Vaughan's Temple in Nature and the Context of "Regeneration"', *Journal of English and Germanic Philology* 74 (1975), 351-60

Peter Thomas, 'The "Desert Sanctified": Henry Vaughan's Church in the Wilderness', in *Sacred Text – Sacred Space: Architectural, Spiritual and Literary Convergences in England and Wales*, edited by Joseph Sterrett and Peter Thomas (Brill, Leiden and Boston 2011), pp.163-91

John N. Wall, *Transformations of the Word: Spenser, Herbert, Vaughan* (University of Georgia Press, 1988). See Chapter 4, pp.273-365.

Graeme J. Watson, 'The Temple in "The Night": Henry Vaughan and the Collapse of the Established Church', *Modern Philology* 84 (1986), 144-61

Robert Wilcher, 'Henry Vaughan and the Church', *Scintilla* No. 2 (1998), 90-104

Robert Wilcher, 'Henry Vaughan, Jeremy Taylor, Edward Sparke, and the Preservation of the Anglican Communion', *Scintilla* No. 12 (2008), 141-59

Robert Wilcher, 'Exile in Breconshire: The Double Displacement of Henry Vaughan', *Scintilla* No. 15 (2011), 119-28

Helen Wilcox, '"Selves in Strange Lands": Autobiography and Exile in mid-seventeenth-century England', in *Early Modern Autobiography: Theories, Genres, Practices*, edited by Ronald Bedford, Lloyd Davis and Philippa Kelly (University of Michigan Press, Ann Arbor 2006), pp. 131-59

Rowan Williams, *Christian Imagination in Poetry and Polity: Some Anglican Voices from Temple to Herbert* (Oxford: SLG Press, 2004); and 'The Archbishop on George Herbert and Henry Vaughan' (28 March 2007, text on his website)

See also the *Scintilla* articles by Peter Thomas and Wynn Thomas in the reading lists for Chapters 1 and 3.

Herbert's poems are quoted from *The English Poems of George Herbert*, edited by Helen Wilcox (Cambridge University Press, 2007).

Chapter Five: Henry Vaughan and Nature

David Crane, 'The Poetry of Alchemy and the Alchemy of Poetry in the Work of Thomas and Henry Vaughan', *Scintilla* No. 1 (1997), 115-22

Ross Garner, *Henry Vaughan: Experience and the Tradition* (Chicago: University of Chicago Press, 1959). See especially pp.113-27.

Louise Guiney, 'An Oxford Poem by Herbert Vaughan', *The Academy*, no.2034 (29 April 1911), pp.510-11.

Diane Kelsey McColley, 'Water, Wood, and Stone: The Living Earth in Poems of Vaughan and Milton', in *Of Paradise and Light* (2004), pp. 269-91

Glyn Pursglove, '"Winged and free": Henry Vaughan's Birds', in *Of Paradise and Light* (2004), pp.250-68

Alan Rudrum, 'Henry Vaughan's "The Book": A Hermetic Poem', *AUMLA* 16 (1961), 161-66

Alan Rudrum, 'The Influence of Alchemy in the Poems of Henry Vaughan', *Philological Quarterly* 49 (1970), 469-80

Alan Rudrum, 'An Aspect of Vaughan's Hermeticism: The Doctrine of Cosmic Sympathy', *Studies in English Literature* 14 (1974), 129-38

June Sturrock, '"Cock-crowing"', *Scintilla* 5 (2001), 152-8

Robert Wilcher, '"Thalia" and the "Father of Lights": Nature and God in the Works of Henry Vaughan and Thomas Vaughan', *Scintilla* No. 16 (2012), 9-36

Robert Wilcher, 'Henry Vaughan and the Poetry of Trees', *Scintilla* No. 14 (2010), 28-50

Chapter Six: Henry Vaughan the Physician

Donald R. Dickson, 'Henry Vaughan's Medical Library', *Scintilla* No. 9 (2005), 189-209.

F.E. Hutchinson, *Henry Vaughan: Life and Interpretation* (1947). See Chapter 14, 'Henry Vaughan, Doctor in Physic', pp.181-94.

Chapter Seven: The Vaughan Heritage

Helen Ashton, *The Swan of Usk* (Collins, London 1939)

Alice Brown, *Louise Imogen Guiney* (Macmillan, New York 1921)

D.F. Corrigan, *Siegfried Sassoon: Poet's Pilgrimage* (Gollancz, London 1973)

F. Forrest, 'Quiet land of the poet mystic', *Country Life,* 9 July 1964

Revd Alexander Grosart, *The Works in Verse and Prose Complete of Henry Vaughan Silurist* (Fuller Worthies Library, 1871)

Theophilus Jones, *History of Brecknockshire* [1805] (Glanusk edition, 1911)

Roland Mathias, *Anglo-Welsh Literature: An Illustrated History* (Poetry Wales Press, Bridgend 1986)

Jonathan Nauman, 'F.E. Hutchinson, Louise Guiney, and Henry Vaughan', *Scintilla* No. 6 (2002), 135-47

E. Pritchard, 'Gwenllian Morgan (1852-1939)', *Brycheiniog* 12 (1966-67)

Siegfried Sassoon Diaries, 1923-5, edited by R. Hart-Davies (Faber and Faber, London 1985)

Index

page numbers in italics indicate illustrations

Act for the Better Propagation and Preaching of the Gospel of Wales 30, 33, 45
Albury xiii
alchemy xi, xiii, 67
Archer, Rebecca xiii
  Timothy xiii
artists inspired by Henry Vaughan 98-9
Ashton, Helen 95
astrology xi
Aubrey, John 9-10, 17, 80, 84, 88
Awen 9-10

Bayle, François 82
Beeston Castle 18, 20
Bible, the 8, 25, 62, 68
  Old Testament 15, 53
  Song of Solomon, the 14
  Song of Songs 43, 49
biblical themes
  Abel 37
  Adam and Eve xvii
  ark 53
  Balaam 36
  baptism 5
  birds 35
  bondage of the Israelites 37
  community 44
  Elijah fed by ravens 13
  God concealed in cloud and fire 19
  Jacob wrestling 13
  marriage at Cana 14, 15
  parable of the seed 54, 57-9
  prodigal son 62
  Rose of Sharon 46
  trees 12

Bliss, Sir Arthur 94
Blunden, Edmund 77
Boethius, Severinus 29
Book of Common Prayer xii, 30, 35, 44-5, 51
Bray, Horace 97
Brecon Priory 12, 18
  visited by Charles I 19
Brown, Alice 91
Brycheiniog ix

'Cavalier winter' 38, 59
Charles I, King 19, 20, 22, 23, 27, 44
  execution 29, 34-5, 80
Chester 19, 22
Christ, Jesus 6, 15, 27, 44, 63
  crucifixion 48
  mocked by Herod 41-2
  nativity 59-60
  Second Coming 16, 35, 40, 69, 70
church, the 43-60
  closed in Interregnum 9
  desecrated by Puritans 22
  Puritan view of 45
  state of religion in Vaughan's day 15-6
  in Vaughan's work 55-6
churches
  closed to Anglican clergy by Puritans 2, 33, 45
Chymical Club xi
Civil War xi-xii, 17-28, 85
Clarke, W. 92
Cluysenaar, Anne 3, 9-10, 96, *96*, 102
Cradock, Walter 30
Cromwell, Oliver 18, 33
Dafydd ap Gwilym 2, 9

Dafydd ap Llywelyn ix
Davies, Gwendoline and Margaret 97
Denham, Sir John 4
Dickson, Donald 81
Donne, John 62

ecology 8, 77-8
Elgar, Edward 94
Eliot, T.S. 94, 96
Elizabeth, Princess 34
Eltonhead, John 21
eternity 1, 7, 8, 16, 28, 51

Fairfax, Sir Thomas 18
Finzi, Gerald 94

Galen 79, 81-3
Gladstone, William 89
God 68
  Creator 72, 75, 78
  presence of 51
Gregynog Press 97
Griffiths, James Robert 89
Grosart, Revd Alexander 89
Grube, Hermann 82
Guiney, Louise 3, 79, 84, 90, 92-3, *92*
Gwasg Gregynog 97

Habington, William 62
Hamill-Keays, Seamus 99
Harvey, William 80, 83
Hatley, Griffith 34
Heaney, Seamus 96-7
herbal remedies 82-3
Herbert, George ix, xi, 47, 48, 49-50, 62, 85
  The Temple xii, 49, 55
  Revd Matthew x-xi, 31, 45

Sir William ix
hermetic thought xi, 53, 67-8, 72, 78, 79
Hicks-Jenkins, Clive 97-8
Hippocrates 81
Hofer, Wolfgang 82
Holst, Gustav 94
Hooker, Jeremy 96
Horace, Roman poet 38
humours 81-2
Hutchinson, F.E. 79, 93

iatrochemical research xiii, 79
Interregnum, the 29-42

Jeffrys, John 17
Jones, Jenkin 32, 33-4
  Shirley 97
  Theophilus 88
Jonson, Ben 62
Joseph, Joseph 89
Juvenal 12, 62

landscape 1-16
Laugharne, Colonel Rowland 18, 20, 23
Lewes, Thomas 30, 32-3, 34, 37-8
Llangattock x, 31, *31*
  Church *32*, 43, 45
Llangorse Lake 2-3, *3*, 4, *54*
Llansantffraed Church (St Bride's) vii, x, *30, 33*, 43, *46, 47, 48*, 79, 87-8, *87, 88*, 89-90, *95*
Lloyd, John 88
Logan, James 81
  Dr William 81
Lotichius, Johann 82
Lyte, Revd H.F. 89

Macdonald, Robert i, 98
Massingham, H.J. 3
Mathias, Roland 10, 95, *95*
Maynard, Robert 97

medicine 79-86
Metaphysical Poets vii
Miller, Karl 96-7
Moray, Sir Robert xiii
Morgan, David x
  Denise x
  Gwenllian 79, 89-90, 91-2, 92-3, *92*
  William 17
Morris, Lewis 89
music inspired by Henry Vaughan 94
nature 54, 61-78
  as church 51-2
neoplatonism 67
Newton (Trenewydd) Farm x, xiii, 2, 4, 7

O'Hahan, Andrew 96-7
Ovid 62
Oxford University xi

Parliamentarians
  guilt 35
  victory in Civil War 2
Parry, Hubert 94
pastoral poetry 1
Paulli, Simon 82
Paynter, Hilary 97
Pecquet, Jean 82, 83
Penn, William 81
Perrott, John x
Peyer, Johann Conrad 83
poets inspired by Henry Vaughan 93-8
Powell, Thomas x, 30, 34
  Vavasour 30
Poyer, Colonel John 23
prayer 52, 57, 62, 66
Price, Sir Herbert 12, 17, 18
Priory Grove, the 12, *12, 13*
Puritans 29, 30, 32, 38, 40, 61
Directory for the Publique Worship of God 45

Vaughan's view of 47

Randolph, Thomas 62
Red Hen Press 97
Restoration, the xiii
resurrection 64, 65-6
Rhys, Ernest 97
romanticism 10, 70
Royalists 21-2, 30, 34, 40, 44

Saint Paulinus of Nola 62
Sassoon, Siegfried 94, 95
Scintilla 8
Scots 23
Silures 6-7
Sinibaldi, Giovanni 83
Southall, Isobel 93-4
'Swan of Usk' 2, 95
Swete, Revd John 88
Symonds, Richard 20

Talybont-on-Usk 5, 83, 102
Tavener, John 94
Thomas, Peter 99, *99*
Tretower Castle *ix*
Tretower Court ix-x, *x*, 97

Usk
  River x, xiii-xiv, 1-2, *2, 3, 5, 6*, 38-9, 61, 62, 73, 88
  Valley vii, x, 6, 43, 52, 61, 73, 94, 97, 102

Vaughan,
  Catherine xii, xvii, 12, 43
  Charles x
  Dean 92
  Denise x, xiii
  Frances ix
  Gwladys ix
  Henry
    acceptance of death 8, 38
    character 36-7, 42
    in Civil War xi-xii,

18-9, 44
 besieged in Beeston
    Castle 18, 20
 and church, loss of 45,
    46, 51, 55
 death of xiii
 as doctor xiii, 79-86
 grave at Llansantffraed
    xiii, 79, 88, 89, 90-1,
    90, 91, 97, 100
 and grief xvii, 24, 29,
    43, 49, 62, 64-5
 illness 86
 studies law in London
    xi, 17, 61
 at Oxford xi, 61
 marriage xii-xiii
 memorial service vii,
    98, *99*
 obscurity 88-9
 poetic vocation 62
 Royalist 21, 44
 secular poetry 38, 63
 spiritual crisis 29, 31
 theology 10
 works
    on the liturgical year
       50
    Flores Solitudinis xii,
       2, 31
    The Mount of Olives
       xii, 8, 24, 45, 46,
       51, 67
    Olor Iscanus xii, 1, 2,
       19, 34, 45, 80, 88
    *Poems with the Tenth
       Satire of Juvenal
       Englished* 12
    Silex Scintillans xii,
       2, 3, 24, 28, 36-7,
       38, 39-40, 45, 47,
       49, 50, 62, 63, 66,
       67, 68, 73, 74, 78,
       86, 89, 92
    Thalia Rediviva xiii
 Rebecca xiii
 Sir Roger of Bredwardine
    ix
 Thomas (father of Henry)
    x, xiii, 34
 Thomas (twin brother of
    Henry)
    and alchemy xi,
       xiii, 5, 67, 68, 74,
       79
    burial at Albury xiii
    in Civil War xi-xii, 18
    obscurity 88
    rector of Llansant-
       ffraed xi, xiii
    eviction as 30-1, 45
    studies x, xi
    works xii, xiii-xiv
 William (grandfather of
    Henry) ix
 William (brother of
    Henry) x
    death of xii, 23-4,
       25, 28, 43, 62, 63,
       64-5, 66-7, 80
 Vaughan Association vii,
    98
 Vaughan garden 83
 Vaughan Walk vii, 83,
    99-100
 Vaughans of Tretower ix
 Verzascha, Bernhard 83

 Walbeoffe, Charles 17,
    32, 36
 waterfalls 4-5, 7-8, 71-2,
    73
 Watkins, Andrew x
 Wise, Catherine xii, xvii,
    12, 43
    Elizabeth xiii
    Richard xii
 Wordsworth, William xv

Index of Henry Vaughan's poems

Affliction (I) 8, 84-85

Begging (II) 86
The Bird 9
The Book 73, 77-78
The British Church 47-49

Christ's Nativity (II) 59-60
Church Service 50
Cock-crowing 68-69
The Constellation 25-27, 53

The Dawning 15-16
The Dedication 6
Distraction 70

Elegy on the Death of Mr R. Hall, Slain at Pontefract 23
An Elegy on the Death of Mr R.W. 19
L'Envoy 37
An Epitaph Upon the Lady Elizabeth 34-5

Fair and young light! xvi-xvii
To His Retired Friend, an Invitation to Brecknock 20-22

I walked the other day (to spend my hour) 63-67
The Importunate Fortune 36

Joy of my life! while left me here 4

The King Disguised 22

The Men of War 41-42

Midnight 5
The Morning-Watch 9, 52-53, 55-57
The Mutiny 36-37
To My Worthy Friend, Master T. Lewes 37-38

To the Pious Memory of C.W. Esquire 32
The Proffer 39-40

Quickness 6

Regeneration 4, 62-63
Religion 12-14
Retirement (I) 53
The Retreat xiv-xv
Rules and Lessons 35, 70

The Seed Growing Secretly 54-55, 57-59
The Shower (I) 4
Silence and stealth of days 24-5

They are all gone into the world of light! 7, 27-8
The Timber 75-77

Upon a Cloak Lent Him by Mr J. Ridsley 20
Upon the Priory Grove, His Usual Retirement 11-12

Vanity of Spirit 73-75

The Water-fall 4, 7-8, 71-73
White Sunday 36
The World (I) 7